Also by Jack Underwood

Happiness
A Year in the New Life

NOT
EVEN
THIS

Jack Underwood

Poetry, Parenthood
& Living Uncertainly

corsair

CORSAIR

First published in Great Britain in 2021 by Corsair

1 3 5 7 9 10 8 6 4 2

Copyright © 2021 by Jack Underwood

The moral right of the author has been asserted.

A CIP catalogue record for this book
is available from the British Library.

ISBN 978-1-4721-5608-2

Typeset in Garamond by M Rules
Printed and bound in Great Britain by Clays Ltd, Elcograf S.p.A.

Papers used by Corsair are from well-managed forests
and other responsible sources.

Corsair
An imprint of
Little, Brown Book Group
Carmelite House
50 Victoria Embankment
London EC4Y 0DZ

An Hachette UK Company
www.hachette.co.uk

www.littlebrown.co.uk

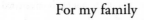

For my family

PREFACE

Not Even

Claims on knowledge are not made through the banishment of uncertainty, but by venturing towards it; answers include their questions; the further you travel into the known, the closer you get to its edges.

For four years, I tried to write a book about uncertainty. It was an unwieldy and potentially endless subject. The more I came to know through my research, the more my lack of knowledge revealed itself.

Every time I entered the forecourts of a new specialism my workaday ignorance was exposed; and the more I sought uncertainty, the more I was forced to see my own life as something corralled into a conceivable and continuous wad through the habitual denial and dampening of reality in all directions.

The brain, with its particular and peculiar evolution, is fundamentally limited in its scope. It does not seem that way. But there are things we can apprehend and then things we cannot, and never will. We may sharpen our different languages, improve the accuracy of the tools with which we measure and explore, but we are always learning inwardly, conceiving more and more within the range of the conceivable. Even when looking outwards, our business is refinement; we are knocking on the inner sides of a hull. Beyond that, and forever – the unknowable.

As a poet, I am relatively familiar with these working conditions. After all, the unknowable exerting its negative presence gives rise to the sublime, which poets have always pursued deliberately. Poets are drawn to the unknowable because it is there that we might test and reckon with our machinery, to have our minds re-blown in glass. Without the unknowable there would be no poetic futile reaching; no mooning around on the platform before the castle, spoken to by ghosts; no common endeavour or homely reminder of the void in the room; no gawping at our hands just to feel the shock of our proximity to one another when finally we look up; no horizon to the event; no shoring of lines against the white space around them; no shoring of that space against the rest of the world; no maddening, soluble 4 a.m. quarry; no singing in search of the song; no sympathetic group work; no animal in the habitat of language; no poems.

Philosophers and critical theorists have documented this uncertain predicament for just as long as poets, and they have named it better, and with rigour, review and citation. It feels conceited to even defer to that greater tradition. I am not a scholar. I have read an armful of their books at best, and could not relay, recite or paraphrase what I have read. Nevertheless, I know my own thoughts are in debt. It would also be dishonest not to acknowledge that theory and philosophy have not so much changed my life, as shown it to me. I am happy to be sentimental about it. If I have anything to add, then it comes from the back of that vast peloton. The feminist epistemologies of Lorraine Code, in particular, have given me more of a sense of what it means to be person (a knower, among other knowers) than the work of perhaps any other writer, including the poets. Gratitude and deference do not cover it; but they will have to do.

If uncertainty has already been so widely accounted for elsewhere, why reinvent the wheel? The question is an accusation. And whenever it was asked of me, directly or indirectly, I did not have an answer. It was my colleague, Nell Stevens, who reminded me that

'Reinventing the wheel' is a pretty good description of what writers do!
And anyway, the wheel would've been a shit invention
if we were only allowed one of them.

And I thought, That's true. We will always need another love poem, another death poem. Uncertainty is not going anywhere, because it is our home. I believe that. And I believe that poetry proves it too. What philosophy and theory have taught me, poetry has allowed me to reoccupy: that words and their meanings are reproduced between us; that the definition of a word arises not from its singular presence as a term but from the recession of all other terms around it, lifting it momentarily into relief, into context; that etymology is the story of a word it has already outgrown; that language does not pour out of me, but is something I have entered, and now I deflect and discover the character and shape of myself by its passing; that meaning is evidence of one's intention to mean, but never exactly what one intends; that meaning is nothing at all without the guesswork and goodwill and hopefulness of humanity, which is eroded when we pretend the situation is otherwise; that knowledge is a remade thing and includes the knower in its making; that the making of the known carries, therefore, an attendant moral responsibility; that we should be careful in our making and remaking; that feelings exist more factually and materially than the names we might give

3

to them; that names are inadequate and always withhold as much as they hold of a thing.

The uncertain knowledge that a poem extends to us is a beckoning home. It is certainty, reason, logic, knowing, that require all the energy, all the desperate rigging up. It is all so exhausting, this life of logical refusal. We deserve to allow ourselves to not know. So I kept going with my research, that it might provoke and tilt at the habits of reason, because I wanted to offer uncertainty to others as respite. And then I became a father.

*

Before our daughter was born, I used to imagine what fatherhood would be like. My fantasies did not include the constant work of parenthood. Or the realisation that the work will never be done. You realise round about week three or four that there is no weekend coming: there is only the child, and love and worry, today and tomorrow, for the rest of your life. I looked at my own parents and felt like a fool, like a child. I had not seen the literal hours and hours of cleaning up after me, teaching me, the years of care and patience, their kindness, their fear, their grief at my need to outgrow them, their grief at their need to never be outgrown. I suddenly saw them in terms of that work, and I felt ashamed. I didn't know what the fuck I had been on about, that's how I felt. And then I looked at my own child, beginning at her beginning, and it shocked me, how habitual and calcified and brutish I was by comparison. There I was, her *father*, continuing to produce my little life story, its tangible, workable, rolling scenario, walking around inside it like I owned the fucking place. And so, humble and shaken, I underwent an adjustment. It took a while. Perhaps two years. But at some point I stopped writing my book about uncertainty and started writing *this* book about uncertainty instead: a book for her, to her.

I have no general thesis about parenting. My experiences of

4

fatherhood do not somehow transcend the particularities of my social and political world. I am straight, white, middle class, with a relatively normative gender identity; hardly a neutral position from which to make universal claims. Children are various people, and the parental relationship you have with your specific child-person is precisely particular. Even between the two parents of the same child, things are so different. I have largely excluded the experiences of Hannah, my 'co-parent', from this book, partly out of respect for her privacy, but mainly because it would be absurd and insulting to pretend for a second that I understand the experience or extent of the work of her motherhood. I don't. I look up at it, like a penguin at an icebreaker vessel. I try to be useful and kind and above all to show my gratitude, and I love her.

In order to write a book about parenting and uncertainty from the point of view of a poet, I have had to find my form along the way. *Not Even This* is an essay, or essays, and at times it is a poem, a letter, a space for play, a space for confiding. Sometimes I lean on analogy to make connections between ideas, but not always explicitly or with a particular conclusion in mind beyond that which a metaphor situates between two things by drawing together their likenesses. Sometimes I lean more heavily on my research, and I apologise in advance to the specialists in those fields who may find my descriptions of certain phenomena to be simplistic; I have tried to honour accuracy as best I can while keeping a more general readership in mind. I have also tried to write with honesty about fatherhood, but the last three years have been very tiring, and I did not take many notes.

I.

LONG LIVE PATIENCE

You are five weeks old. You weigh about four kilograms, the same as our cat. Your vision can only draw objects into focus if they lie within forty centimetres of your face. The rest is background. Your sense of day, night, your body and what lies beyond it, is vague. I am not sure whether you are able to isolate your own voice from the rest of sound, whether your cry is something you feel that you make, or if it is suddenly just there, part of the world.

I watch your face, errantly exploring its possible positions and combinations, and I think I can see recognition taking hold. Not of me, or the room, but of yourself, being here. I know that you are already beginning to impress your memory onto the present, stopping you from existing in a constant state of spooling, endless newness. And we, as your parents, are a central part of that impression of continuity: our faces arriving above your cot and leaving again, waking, feeding, changing, sleeping, not sleeping, the light of the 4 a.m. television, muted with subtitles, the patterns of our shift work across this bleary, newborn time zone, daily ceremonies ... these are your first worldly repetitions, the first structures by which you navigate your presence, or predict and prepare for whatever sensation comes next; in other words, your first language.

The brain is not a general-purpose device. [...] Human concepts and human language are not random or arbitrary; they are highly structured and limited, because of the limits and structure of the brain, the body, and the world.

– George Lakoff and Rafael E. Núñez

Your fluency in this language is absolute, because you have never known another way of measuring yourself against the passing of time. We all started off this way: a tiny pool of repetitions imposed upon the present, giving our novel lives the impression of similarity, when in truth, no one has ever been anywhere before, despite the mind's invigilation.

Then the tiny pool floods out and deepens. We continue to draw our past into the present. But we also begin to imagine alternative versions of events. We triangulate and rerun. We edit and fantasise. And we rehearse our futures too, catastrophic or heroic, the terrible accident, the narrow escape, the *mot juste*, the acceptance speech ... The outside world, various and ready, runs parallel to the creativity of our inner lives, each tramline steering the other. And somehow language mediates. Or perhaps it rescues us from meaninglessness: modulating what we feel and imagine with its concepts, its theoretical frameworks. Language lays its names over and across the present like the eastings and northings and contours of a map. It gives shape and reason, a stable sense of relativity within its system, and a relationality with the world.

By adulthood, language and reality are hard to tell apart. The tiny pool of our early repetitions has become a great wide lake of terms and laws to apply ... there is so much language to our consciousness that we scarcely move beyond those waters, while our desires and impulses coalesce in the unknown depths and eddies, convecting in the dark: those drowned voices, hidden

8

from memory, that rise and find us in our sleep, half remembered, rarely understood.

This will happen to you too. With your 'highly structured and limited' brain, you will learn like the rest of us to recognise the feeling of *being* as a pattern, and part of me mourns this loss for you. You're still so *beginning*! The slide into a conceptual present feels so brutal. Perhaps it is the inevitability of it; as if you could live some more authentic, less moderated existence instead, and your wild, contingent, newborn way of being in the world might be preserved or protected; as if you will one day grow up and demand to know why I didn't save you from language, this dulled, violently categorical version of being alive.

*

Three months have passed. Your world is no longer encountered as a diffuse, contingent mass of stimuli hailing you from within and without, but as a collection of things in relation to yourself. I can see already how insidiously, how without thinking, the words and symbols for these things will arrive next, as if they were not sounds and shapes that we taught you to make, over and over, but somehow part of the things themselves:

> We must consider ourselves as a symbolic, semantic class of life
> [. . .] the word is not the thing.
>
> – Alfred Korzybski

Your brain, thoroughly calibrated by thousands of years of evolution to choose the efficiency and safety of finding repetition over the vulnerability of living in a world perpetually new, is readying itself for the nameable world. In time you will simply accept the limited version, its habitual roll call, and so you will reduce your reality in order to know it.

9

A door.
A tree.
Water.

*

Now I am wishing the days away. In such a hurry. I want to know you, and to be known by you more and more. I want you to be more *arrived*. Why does this part take so long? I want you to speak to me, to pass the symbols back and forth, so that it feels as if we are, yes, both *here* – not just here in the world, but in the world and in language simultaneously: a place where love and knowledge can be declared with a reassuring sense of ongoing permanence. I want you to meet me *here*, where the words are!

*

Daddy. A name. A handle. A contract. And it is a mad wish, really, to want to be named that way, because if anything I am lost in its prevalence. It is only a rain cloud to stand in. But such contracts are all we have to know one another.

*

But does language really reduce our contact with reality? All at once, in a gasp of thought, it seems only to complicate the world, to open it up to us; there is so much of it, and it takes so many different forms, with its signs and gestures and ceremonies. How miraculous that it might bring you closer to the surface of yourself and to us, bring you *here* to me. Every day we say it: *bring her to me, give her to me, let me take her,* and doesn't language do that more than anything else? An equal miracle to being alive and witnessing another life begin is being able to make life comprehensible. It is miraculous that we possess the faculties to simplify reality for ourselves in this way.

In otherwise total darkness
there was a handle

10

became my hand

and I was very somewhere

when suddenly I took it.

*

Then, today, I looked at you and thought about all the repression and the burying that human beings attend to in exchange for this workable coherence within ourselves and with the world. I thought about how we burn and fuse the brain's shorter routes to learn, how we teach ourselves with the pain that the body makes for us, its harsh replies, to expect the ground to be hard, to expect radiators, oven doors, cups of tea to be hot, to fear love and connection that might one day be lost ... You cannot even swallow solid food yet, or deliberately drop an object ... Your mind's sums of reduction will also be your mode of survival; without them, where would any of us be? Not here at all.

*

I searched online to find out how far you can see. There was no average visual range given for a five-month-old baby, but I did discover that you now have the fundamentals of depth perception. You can experience distance. It makes me imagine the time when our faces must have simply bubbled up before you.

I also learned that the central visual range of the human eye is only 5 degrees, and that most of our 120 degrees of vision is peripheral. It is the eye's narrow progress across an object that accumulates a sense of its whole, in the form of memory; we rarely see anything in one go. Most of what we 'see' is what we remember. I go and run the tap. What am I looking at?

We do not think real time. But we live it, because life transcends intellect.

– Henri Bergson

*

11

I distract myself and do not stop
to remember my clothes
are not my body, or
to listen to paintings.
Am I even in a room, or just following
its story to the next confusion
like my weight on the floor?
I want to tell you
there is a necessary loneliness
in anything unverified;
loneliness is anything unverified.
It's 4:21 a.m. and I have taken you
to the sofa so your mother can sleep,
the television flickers blue
with the sound down
subtitles landing the story in chunks
while you shut yourself in sleep
and I am not lonely
but laying to waste
the rest of my life
over my shoulder
to be here this way
with you like a habit
like a knack or a lock
like the downturn or narrowing
on my face,
which I hardly ever check
to read, daughter,
in a line of cars at night,
or a line of thoughts preceding,
and when I do, I lie.

*

12

The word is not the thing, but the thing is not the thing either. Not really. Central visual range 5 degrees. Most of human experience involves sensorial foregrounding, and narrative imagination. Being is a creative act. We only have five apprehensive, sensory faculties to work with, and they are deployed with efficiency in mind, not extra-human, fundamental truth. These are not new observations:

Nothing can be known; not even this.

– Carneades of Cyrene

We live within our structures and limits and the brain is not going to evolve any time soon. *Here* we all are, regardless.

*

Your vulnerability overwhelms me. I'm worried all the time now. I worry about the size of this love that needs attending to. How it pushes at us. How far away we seem from each other, all three. How trapped within ourselves we are.

But I also worry that, in pursuit of a world we can know and share, in which we might articulate our love and know each other better, we must also lay so much to waste. I mean all of humankind. What if, being here according to our certain, limited terms, human beings are habitually laying so much to waste that it is compromising the sustainability of life on this planet?

What if mass-scale human cognitive and apprehensive reduction of the kind that allows us to experience reality, and each other, has outgrown the practicalities of our survival as a species?

I worry that in order to live *here*, where love might be felt and communicated, we too readily ignore the significance of our fundamentally limited scope as discerning agents, and that now our inherent cognitive wastefulness is existentially dangerous. Seven billion people, including you now, laying waste, all of the time, in order to know a reality according to the finite limits of the human mind; on such a scale there must surely be some great consequence to this limited, dominant version. Irreversible climate change is one: a tangible symptom of the human mind's reductive sickness.

> (only) A door.
> (only) A tree.
> (only) Water.

But some of us are laying more to waste than others. Some of us are so deep in our certain limited language of knowing that we have forgotten the gap between the word and the thing altogether.

Some of us refuse the unknowable, say that it is a weakness to not know. Some of us violently enforce our simplified sense of coherence upon others, in spite of the clear variety of experiences. Yes, some of us are laying more to waste. The literal, the self-evident, the obvious, the supposedly universally known ... These are blunt objects. I'm not worried, I'm scared.

I am scared that even if significant necessary changes are made to prolong life on our planet, the brute wastefulness of knowing, structured and limited, cannot be significantly changed. Knowledge and how we make it are an inescapable feature of being here, an inevitable human tragedy:

Horatio: And let me speak to th' yet unknowing world
How these things came about. ~~So shall you hear~~
~~Of carnal, bloody and unnatural acts,~~
~~Of~~ accidental judgements, casual slaughters;
~~Of~~ deaths put on by ~~cunning and~~ forced cause;
~~And, in this upshot,~~ purposes mistook

Let us say that it is not inevitable. Let us ask how we can be *here* less violently, prone to fewer 'casual slaughters'. Can we know less wastefully? Maybe uncertainty can be a positive position in knowledge, like Keats's 'negative capability', which he defines as

> when man is capable of being in uncertainties, Mysteries, doubts, without any irritable reaching after fact & reason.

Perhaps we can unburden ourselves from the pursuit of final, absolute truths and reach for knowledge as provisional, empathetic evidence of our shared desire and effort to be here:

> There probably is no absolute authority, no practice of all practices or scheme of all schemes. Yet it does not follow that conceptual schemes, practices, and paradigms are radically idiosyncratic or purely subjective. Schemes, practices, and paradigms evolve out of communal projects of inquiry. To sustain viability and authority, they must demonstrate their adequacy in enabling people to negotiate the everyday world and to cope with the decisions, problems, and puzzles they encounter daily.
> – Lorraine Code

'Decisions, problems, and puzzles'... you float on a raft of those – your eyes wide and bright as new pound coins, your fingers always in your mouth – but I don't know if I am coping well. No absolute authority is to hand, for either of us. This is a communal project of enquiry and I am trying very hard to demonstrate my adequacy.

*

Poems are communal projects of enquiry. I could stick by that definition. They are useful for their particular kindness and their peculiar scrutiny. As a conceptual scheme, poetry offers uncertain knowledge, it brings complexity within reach, allows a question to reverberate the room. A poem asks you to be an imaginative and intellectual participant in its activity, rather than a passive receiver of information. A poem asks you what it means, even as it tells you. A poem is a situation of deliberate intersubjectivity in language: the offer of a meeting place, *here*, where we can be in uncertainty, without 'irritable reaching'.

*

> Each individual reader will fill in the gaps in his own way, thereby excluding the various other possibilities; as he reads, he will make his own decision as to how the gap is to be filled.
>
> – Wolfgang Iser

The meaning of a text, whether literary or not, is not exact. The reader, who might even be the writer, is active in producing meaning, a process which can be spontaneous and impulsive and mysterious, and at the same time policed and regulated ... which is all part of the ongoing process of definition. The word is not the thing, but a thing of its own: makeable, mutable, reliant on rearticulation for the credibility of its exchange. And so our exchanges are offered hopefully, with slippage and blurring in mind; so much rests on trust.

In poems, language is deployed very deliberately as an unfinished material: provisional, equivocal, interpretable, moving, with a need for mutual trust and faith implied by its symbolism or ambiguities. It is because of this uncertain unfinishedness that poetry necessitates our active role in its knowledge-making. And so poetry, as an uncertain knowledge-form, works by welcoming and drawing our daily 'problems and puzzles' into its orbit, reminding us that the brain is not an all-purpose device, that it is natural to be overwhelmed, that the room is always reverberant with newness and the unknowable, and that life is constantly drifting beyond our certain terms.

                                              (only) A door.
                                              (only) A tree.
                                              (only) Water.

Poetry reminds us that language only works at all because we bring ourselves to bear upon it; we enter it together, hopefully, and divine each other by each other's good faith.

I knew all this before you were born. But watching your increasing self-coherence according to the limits and structures of your brain, and watching you enter into language, into continuity, by its divisions and re-impressions, has made me value the poetic ways of knowing the world with a fresh urgency. I mean, I don't know what the fuck is going on. I never did, but now I know I don't. Look at you, for example. Unsolvable. I am your expert and I am dumbfounded. And that's fine. Isn't it? Why am I asking you? You don't know either. But I demand your right to be in uncertainty. I demand your right to know that 'nothing can be known; not even this'. I don't want you to grow up scared of not knowing, but to inhabit it with acceptance, and clarity. I promise I will do my best to find uncertainty for you, and prove it both beautiful and true.

                                              *

                     To question the terms of the contract of waking,
                              to a flooded house and intervention;
                            to communal projects, overwhelmed,
                          encountered daily, long live patience,
                              to know the world less violently,
                                  less wastefully, both hands
                              in the blanket, and eyes in distillation,
                    burning up their clouds, just now latching on.

II.

A SONG ABOUT SINGULARITIES

What are you singing?
I'm singing a song.
But what's your song about?
I don't know.

*

You have become a passionate collector since we bought you the backpack. You have always kept a handful of objects in rotation, items you have taken a particular shine to, that have interested you more deeply than others. But the arrival of the backpack has provided fresh impetus, a reason to collect things as much as a place to put them. So it is no longer the objects themselves that are of interest to you, but the novel fact of your possessing them, your having them to hand, within your remit. These are your belongings and you are playing at making them belong to you.

It must be a new sensation, deliberate ownership ... a little extra electricity in your relation to 'the world's waterspout of objects' as Lorca describes them, each so discrete and phenomenal. There is your tiny sun-blanched snail shell, an acorn, two bits of string, the plastic earrings and the two glass bead necklaces

18

half donated by your mother, four old train tickets, the bright orange corner of a takeaway menu, a set of two keys on a ring (the location of the corresponding locks long forgotten), a postcard from your great-granny, a bedraggled dandelion head, a small magnifying glass from your Christmas stocking, a set of cheap plastic crimping scissors, a spinning top from a cracker, several stones of no remarkable shape or colour, a rolled-up treasure map your mother drew you last week, a wooden wand, a debit card receipt from the off-licence, a large, yellow, waxy leaf from the magnolia tree . . . no hierarchy, no discernible pattern or consistency to the arrangement, which you assemble and disassemble on the floor about you everywhere you go. Come bedtime, everything must be packed away, carried upstairs, then placed on your chest of drawers next to the bed, to be found again in the morning. In the morning, the items are packed and taken downstairs where you begin a new day of judicious governance, demarcating your landscape, organising its distances while sipping your juice and watching cartoons. You are alone in your logic of category and position, muttering as you work, seeming to name the items as you go, or else providing a commentary on your progress.

If you are very tired, you sometimes ask us to help you, and this is a treacherous undertaking, because in such a state you cannot communicate the exact positioning you are after, the angle or relationship or the reasoning behind it. When we fail to satisfy the particularity of your design, which is inevitable, you turn first furious, then inconsolable. Tears before bedtime. A hostage negotiation, in which we are both negotiator and hostage.

Deep breaths. I know, I know, I must make room for you to explain. But come evening, when I have been patient all day and am also very tired, the exact configuration of a piece of string relative to a wooden bowl relative to a plastic dinosaur (is it meant

19

to be drinking from the bowl or washing in it? Is the string part of this? Is it the dinosaur's food?) are not specifics I am deeply invested in. I have to dig deep into my reserves. I can see that the little control you have over your world has been overthrown by these minor misalignments. You are so distraught and frustrated.

For as long as you have called out to us in want, in confusion, we have tried to meet your demands. The work of our caregiving, our bending to your shape and shade, has been so prevalent that it must surely be imperceptible to you. Now my clumsy, stupid interventions, suddenly arriving from outside of your new thinking, must register like an internal malfunction; you do not understand why I do not understand. Let's start from the top. The dinosaur, where does she go? After five or six minutes, we have them in place: dinosaur, bowl, string, the elements returned to their periodic table . . . and we are both exhausted and united in our relief.

*

I don't consider myself a collector. In fact, I am generally unattached to material things. People tell me I am impossible to buy gifts for because I'm just as happy with one thing as I am another, or nothing at all. Being so ambivalent means that I can also forget to say thank you, which is awful, so I worry about it, and then, when I do remember, I worry that my thanks will seem too performed, disingenuous, which on a certain level I suppose they are, which is also awful.

It is not just that I'm not invested in objects, but that I am irritated by objects that other people deem to be precious because I fear I'm likely to break them, or lose them, or spill tomato sauce or wine down the front of them, or, more neurotically, fear that I might take a blade or blunt object to them deliberately, driven by a sudden, perverse impulse. Precious things, even those given to me lovingly, feel like a test. It is as if my ability to care and

20

be careful is placed under a scrutiny that seems utterly unjust, given that I don't get any materialist pleasure in exchange, only a dreadful foreboding, a sense that I can only stand to ruin and disappoint.

Before you were born, I knew you would be precious, and I fought against endless dark visions of dropping you, knocking your head against a doorway, tripping up and landing on top of you. I cringed and winced to myself multiple times a day. Unsurprisingly, before you I never enjoyed holding babies; handing them back even after twenty seconds felt like a triumph. The child survived me! It was like that with you for the first few days too. After my turn, feeling your weight leave my arms, I would rise with the elation of the unindicted, free-to-go. Seeing all the casual super-dads on train station platforms or striding across beer gardens with their slings and papooses made me prickle with anxiety, though these are, I am sure, normal feelings for a new parent. That I experience a feeling of triumph taking off a new shirt that has made it through dinner is less usual, I would say. If I have a fondness for objects at all it is for those that are already wearing out. New items are as yet unsullied by use, and old antique items are precious precisely because they have survived so long against the odds, but worn-in objects demand no particular vigilance – T-shirts whose print is fading and seams are stretched, beaten up copies of books, cheap sunglasses, my creaky writing chair that the barber in Hackney let me have for free, its legs held together with a metal hose clip – I can be entrusted with them freely, these old, waning faithfuls, already in need of replacing. And it is a relief. Because I am clumsy and paranoid I live in fear; relief is my favourite emotion.

Was I always like this? As I child I collected frog ornaments. My collection had more than a hundred pieces at its peak, some ceramic, some wood, mostly cheap plastic. I remember I liked the feeling and ceremony of adding to it, one more to the chorus. I must have packed it away during early puberty, out of shame or a lack of interest. When my parents moved house (long after I had left home) the loft was emptied, and I agreed to have them given away or thrown out. They kept a couple of the nice bronze resin ones that I was given as Christmas and birthday presents, and they live in their bathroom now. I pick them up when I visit, but I don't feel any attachment. I haven't collected anything else since, unless you count books, which I accrue rather than pursue. Even then, I'm pretty ambivalent about the editions themselves and I wish I had fewer. A very slow reader, I am hopelessly besieged.

But I do have a drawer in my desk that is full of odd bits and pieces, the hip flask I was given on my eighteenth birthday (a family tradition) and some photos in clip frames I don't have room to display, a harmonica (in the key of A) in its case, three old mobile phones parked up along the edge of the drawer like limousines in a motorcade. There is also the ceramic pot beside the lamp, where I keep a positive pregnancy test, and two peanuts in their shells that Kaveh sent me all the way from New York City. I like to have them. I like to pick them up and say, 'New York City'. And I am proud to have kept the peanuts safe for three years now. I can't see myself throwing the pregnancy test away. But still, there is nothing that I would rush to save in a house fire, or stuff into a suitcase before the tanks roll in. They are just the clog, the mulch, the effluent of the business of living. I know I could start again.

It's not that I'm not sentimental. I think it's more the case that I am too sentimental. I find old batteries funereal. I thank cash machines and postboxes, and sometimes, embarrassingly, lifts as I leave them. I feel I could become attached to anything if I was to idly cast some symbolic importance on it, give it a persona, a name, which I do all the fucking time. When it comes to material objects, relativism is a kind of defence, a healthier, less exhausting outcome than the alternative, which is a meaningful and particular relationship with everything.

*

An obvious analogy occurs: the similarity between the positioning of your miscellaneous objects, and the business of shifting a poem about on a page. Wait, OK, now I understand exactly what you're doing: that need to go back over and over, testing configurations, rehearsing the through-lines and relations ... the muttering and staring into space, and yes, admittedly, when I'm tired and feel that I cannot convey my predicament, or the correct formal arrangement does not materialise I, too, know that inconsolable frustration ... Words have to be right, and in the right order and position.

I pick up your little orange corner of takeaway menu. It is a word as good as any, with its bright, discrete shape and character, retaining a little of the wider history it was torn from; as good as any to carry from room to room, to unpack and repack relative and in response to where it lands or whatever it lands next to. And I understand your need to sit in the middle, laying down your predicament, arranging your poems about you. Your poems *about* you.

*

I am often asked what a poem is 'about' and it always feels reductive, like the person asking the question is demanding I offer an alternative, snappier version with a clearer, more direct meaning – they do not trust the poem, or they do not trust themselves to trust it. But I try to remember that we talk of moving 'about' something to mean *around* it, almost errantly – one strolls about the park, or dances about the room – and how easily, in this sense, a poem can be *about* its subject.

'About' is also used to mean 'approximately'. It qualifies an

23

amount with a caveat, which is a paradox, since something cannot be both a certain amount and an uncertain amount, and again, the way in which a poem might be said to be *about* a tree, for example, appropriately acknowledges the way in which a poem simultaneously measures and approximates its subject.

*

The centre of our galaxy, the Milky Way, is about 26,000 light years away from Earth. It is thoroughly obscured by huge clouds of dust; no information that we could perceive with the naked eye can ever reach us from beyond that vast cosmic weather front.

However, a German astronomer, Reinhard Genzel, turned to the measurement of infrared radiation as a means of exploring the galactic centre, because, although it has a wavelength beyond our visual range, it can penetrate space dust. The highly precise infrared radiation data that Genzel's team collected throughout the 1990s and early 2000s enabled them to measure and eventually chart the velocities and orbits of the stars closest to the galactic centre, and so build a description of what is there. They found a truly extreme environment, where the velocity of the orbiting stars was so great, and the mass of that region so compacted, that there could only be one explanation: our galaxy is organised around a supermassive black hole, Sagittarius A*, with a mass of more than four million times that of our own sun.

Since then, an enormous amount of evidence has been gathered to support the theory that, far from being unique, our galaxy is comparable to our neighbouring large galaxies, in the sense that they, too, have a supermassive black hole at their nucleus.

If all the large galaxies of the universe have a supermassive black hole at their centre, then these huge phenomena, taken together, can be viewed as a grand parliament. Our own municipal representative, Sagittarius A*, has overseen the relatively stable conditions in which all intelligent life that we are aware of has evolved. All human knowledge, activity and experience has derived from the circumstantial conditions created by an object that we humans can never experience directly, and that will always keep the fundamentals of its nature hidden from us.

A black hole is a perfect analogy for uncertainty, for how life and reality 'transcend intellect'. Our entire existence depends upon these points in space where mass is compressed infinitely inwards, to an essentially unreachable centre, unreadable in any of our languages. And yet we know they are there, because of that which they draw into their orbit, which we can read and interpret. Perhaps instead of speaking of *objects* at the centre of large galaxies, we could say that such a galaxy describes to us the uncertainty at its centre, by the activity it performs *about* it.

*

You don't know what your song is about?
No.
And what are you singing about now?
I am singing about a song.

*

I want to live more uncertainly, and to understand uncertainty as a fundamental feature of how I know the world. I want to be less wasteful and reductive through it. And I want you to have a fuller, more profound experience of being alive by also being able to be in uncertainty. So I have started to try and ask myself not what I know, but what do I know *about*? How much do I know *about* it? I have tried not to think of facts, or pieces of information, as knowledge itself, but as material being drawn into the orbit of what I don't or can't know. It helps me visualise the way I know things and, more importantly, to understand that even the things I do feel I know *about*, are not irrefutable chunks. The agreed facts and dates and names have only become the fixed coordinates through a process of argument and debate and experimentation, but knowledge itself involves a further correlative enterprise, something more creative and intuitive, like the way an eye moves and gathers its story, each point drawn into the shape of a constellation, or like pointillist dots that render a picture only when one stands back and places them in relation to each other. Just like Genzel did. Just like you do.

*

In order to understand what a black hole is, it is necessary to first understand in basic terms some of the principal ideas of Einstein's general theory of relativity. Einstein's theory explains that an object with mass distorts spacetime around it, which we experience as gravitational force of attraction. Often, physicists use a 2D analogy of a trampoline and an object sitting on it, where spacetime is the fabric of the trampoline, and the object, let us say a daughter, represents mass. The daughter's massive presence bends the fabric. It creates a curvature of the spacetime trampoline that she is sitting in the middle of. Were you to introduce other items, say the contents of the daughter's rucksack, to the trampoline, they would each be drawn towards her at the centre by the bending of the fabric, where they would finally collide with the daughter. This is what we call gravity. As Carlo Rovelli puts it:

The gravitational field is not diffused through space; the gravitational field is that space itself. This is the idea of the theory of general relativity. Newton's 'space', through which things move, and the 'gravitational field' are one and the same thing.

But how far can the trampoline bend? What if the daughter was the size of a marble but had the mass of a million daughters? Then the fabric of the trampoline would be pulled into a severe funnel. This severe funnelling of spacetime is what a black hole is. Except, in reality we live in a 4D universe, so the funnelling is not happening downwards, but inwards from all directions. The 'funnel' is a vast region of spacetime curving increasingly inwards, towards the black hole at the centre who is imploding into herself. At a certain distance from the centre of the black hole, even light is unable to escape the sheer extent of her inward curvature, and beyond this 'event horizon' no information escapes. This is what is meant by the 'blackness' of the black hole.

It is theorised that an inner horizon exists, where matter entering the black hole meets the matter already violently imploding, and this is thought to be one of the most extreme environments in the universe.

Physicists call the centre of a black hole a 'singularity'; the general theory of relativity no longer works there. We don't have a description for the forces and their physical relationship that coheres with the rest of reasonable thought. The word 'singularity' derives from the Latin *singularis*, which means 'alone', as in unique, which I find very poetic, in the sense that it might also describe a person, say, a daughter, and how their uniqueness is something we can see from the particular activity and arrangement they enact upon the world around them.

I also like that the word 'singularity' contains the word 'sing', because song is what happens when ordinary language bends and, by its curvature, is able to describe a phenomenon beyond reason.

*

Singularities have existed in theoretical terms for over a hundred years, but the problem is that the maths of a singularity describes an illogical situation in reality: how can mass be compacted into an infinitely small point in space with infinitely great gravity? As Michio Kaku explains:

> To a mathematician infinity is simply a number without limit; to a physicist it's a monstrosity!

This description is not compatible with the physical universe as we otherwise know or encounter it. How can all the mass of a black hole be contained within a space that takes up no space at all? At the point of a singularity,

> space makes no sense; it means the collapse of everything we know about the physical universe. In the real world there is no such thing as infinity; therefore there is a fundamental flaw in the formulation of Einstein's theory.
>
> – Michio Kaku

Mathematicians have tried to apply the laws of quantum mechanics to the problem of the singularity. After all, quantum mechanics provides a mathematical description of the world on an atomic scale that experiment has shown to be astonishingly accurate, even though we cannot encounter that world directly through our senses (more on this later). But singularities are not only small, they also have a huge mass and therefore exert a huge gravitational force, which is not the case with the atoms and particles of the quantum world; a singularity described in quantum terms returns the result of infinite infinities, which to a physicist must be a monstrous monstrosity! So now physicists are searching for a theory of quantum gravity, a reconciliation of quantum mechanics and general relativity, to accommodate both the infinitesimal scale of singularities, and the massive forces at play. In the meantime the singularity remains an enigma, a contradiction, an uncertainty, a little poem at the centre of everything.

*

Poems and black holes have a lot in common. Both have a singularity, for instance. Poems also keep their centres hidden, and like black holes they do not return a final value but indicate a place that falls outside of the usual laws of the language we use to describe them. The critic Cleanth Brooks wrote of 'the heresy of paraphrase', the act of describing a poem outside of the terms of its particular configuration; a poem is precisely *these words in this order, laid out like this*, and so it follows that to paraphrase what a poem is saying – using different terms, in a different order – is a heretical act.

On the whole, most people understand that the value of a poem comes largely out of an acceptance of its singularity, an acceptance of its uncertain value, which does not, after all, prohibit you from enjoying the feeling of being drawn into it, the pull of its gravity. The aftermath of a good poem is not unlike the physicist's infinity outcome: a monstrosity according to the standard rules and definitions ... and yet, there it is, churning away in space, a small, massive song. Such an outcome is not an intellectual or emotional impasse, but a dynamic form of obscurity, to be gnawed upon indefinitely.

Like Genzel and his team, we can identify a poem's meaningfulness not by looking directly at it, but by charting the material, the feelings, associations, images and memories that it draws towards its singularity: words undergoing extreme curvature, compacting into a kind of knowledge that after a certain point cannot be apprehended from outside this dense and dark configuration.

> The mathematical 'singularity' of infinite density and space–time curvature that supposedly lies at the hearts of black holes is an admission of defeat.
> – 'Black Hole Breakthrough', *New Scientist*, 20 April 2019

Or we might say that a poem is an admission of defeat for language as we normally use it to describe the world, language collapsing, densifying, increasing its gravity, summoning a further field of associations and testing our sense of relativity. Or perhaps we are the singularity at the centre of a poem, our personhood, our predicament causing the collapse of language *about* us, our uncertainty a place of infinite gravity.

*

I admit defeat. To the universe
and walls of dust.
Nothing can be known; not even
the subject of the song, subject
to its curvature, subject at the centre,
you, daughter,
singular one and song, your
gravity your gravity; everything you touch

an ornament to its articulation.
Your world arranged about you,
like a crater
on the surface of the room.

III.

THE NEITHERNESS AND SINGULARITY OF SAINT JOAN

On closer investigation it can seem, unnervingly, as if Joan's star might collapse into a black hole. [. . .] The accounts we have, in other words, don't straightforwardly build into a coherent and internally compatible whole.

— Helen Castor, *Joan of Arc: A History*

Throughout your first two years, I have often forgotten that you are a girl, that is, I have found myself remembering. At first, when you were a newborn, it was hard to conceive of you as human. I knew to expect a baby smaller than the bruisers and silkworms I saw in their prams in town, but when you arrived you were unbelievably tiny. If I could travel back in time I would still be surprised. In an early photo, your body rests comfortably along the length of my forearm. 6 lbs 9 oz. I had it memorised. It's one of those things that people always ask, and I reported it like the result of a recent sporting fixture. Your pre-gestural movements were those of a body exploring the novelty of its dimensions, with little discernible purpose or intention, and there was an animatronic quality about you; you seemed unrealistic. You were always sleeping or feeding or puking or excreting your strange gunky meconium, black as seaweed, and with your baggy, pink, suede skin, you looked larval, alien. And when you cried it was not like hearing or seeing an adult or child human cry. It was like an alarm going off. And you had no idea why you were sounding it either. We were left to run our own fraught diagnostics, offering you what we could and trying not to freak out.

God, that cry. Like a pulled tooth, held into the air. It would jolt my chest into a gallop, a shooting pain, a full-body wince. Often I would wake to find myself already out of bed, cot-side, reaching down towards it in the dark, my mind a house fire of scrambled sleep and sound. Such relief when you fell quiet again. There was no peace like your closed, intent sleep. A sleep precisely as heavy as you were in our arms. But I carry that cry in my memory like the tenderness beneath a scar. Even now, at night, your voice finds me like a current down a wire, and I am stepping straight from my dream into your room, my T-shirt somehow on, though inside out, the rescue already underway, preceding thought and consciousness.

Then there were the moments when you were awake and alert and calm, and those were our meeting place. *What are you doing?* I'd whisper to you, your hands grabbing at the air, the way a person might clench their fist after putting on a glove. Sometimes I'd help you locate my index finger so that together we could test your grip and gauge how real you were. Close encounters, the room tightening with these bold reassurances of our presence to one other.

*

I remember that one Boxing Day, when I was a teenager, my parents persuaded me, hungover and in need of some fresh air, to join them for a walk across the fields beyond the village. We reached a farm track where the wheels of a tractor had made long parallel puddles which had frozen over in the cold of the season. As we followed the path, Dad methodically cracked them with a walking stick. *What are you doing?* I asked in protest, because vaguely complaining was my mode for the occasion. *Well . . . because it's what you do, isn't it*, Dad replied, refusing to indulge my preciousness about it, which he could tell wasn't genuine anyway. We kept on walking, and I started cracking a few puddles myself after that, ambivalent, cursory, proving the thesis by testing it: *it's what you do, isn't it.* I don't think Dad intended to be profound – he might just as well have said *because I feel like it* – but it strikes me now that he was not just suggesting it as an act of absent-mindedness: to act on impulse once is impulsive, but act on the same impulse repeatedly and you're dealing with an ongoing investigation, contingent intent: it's what you *do*, not what you *did*. And it's true. We probe, poke and disturb out of curiosity, but also because we measure our presence by that disturbance. It gives us personhood.

So it was with you, grabbing, smearing, knocking things over, putting things in your mouth. A salty wooden brick. A smooth rubber ring. The fur of a teddy's leg. And then, after six months, a piece of banana. Imagine being a baby, introducing a piece of banana into your mouth for the first time: it must be like bringing up the lights of an opera house. A dramatic act of self-location.

We tend to think of ourselves as whole and complete agents, certain of the borders and boundaries where we meet the world, but that is a lie: it is what *you do*; we are permeable things, located by our uncertain interactions with whatever we encounter.

*

A girl. Huh. The idea bobs like a cork. I had forgotten again. Do you remember that you are a girl? I forget I am a man all the time.

I always have my bigger fish to fry. It seems that way for you too. Do you feel you possess a gender enough to forget and remember that you have it? Is gender something one even possesses?

Sometimes you practise your girlishness. I mean literally, in front of the mirror. You raise your shoulder to your chin and look upwards in a coy shrug. I use the word 'practise' because you repeat the poses; it is a rehearsal, and there is an element of assessment to the way you observe yourself, which infers a desire to cohere with an ideal. You are taking instruction, but from where? I don't want you to cohere with an ideal. Ideals are precisely theoretical, and trying to actualise them, or feeling the need to, is a cruelty towards oneself that no amount of practice can alleviate. But how can I protect you from this cruelty when I'm the one reading the movements of your body as 'girlish'? I'm the one weighing you up according to a binary idea of gender. Is it a sense that I myself am guilty of complicity that unsettles me? That you are doing all this to cohere with a version of the world we have raised you to know? Is there any other world we might raise you in but our own, and its limitless anterior of cleaving? Should I stop you? Like the first few times I turned the television off or over when the cartoons drew you a likeness too cartoonish. You seem to take pleasure in achieving some proximity to the ideal, even though that same idealism sets you up to fail. What answer do I have, as your dad, to that pleasure?

The specifics of your sexual anatomy are beside the point of your personhood, which is already so radical and spacious that it fills up every room you enter. Who you might one day be able to or want to procreate with is your business. But the world as it stands will summon your dormant reproductive organs to give a primary account of your ontology. Even though you are only two. It is perverse to think of you in those terms at all, let alone think of it as a fundamental characteristic of how you might understand yourself. You should not be subjected to this binary, sexualized cleaving when you might never want to be part of the Great Reproductive Economy. It feels creepy, and like an attack on your future. The pink noise everywhere. I would try to forget again and again that you are a girl, if I felt that it might help you retain the full futurity of your personhood. Where does my jurisdiction end? Where do you begin? I should be doing more. I will. I promise.

Feminism taught me to contest the limits of patriarchal language and imagination, and help to resist its erasures and violences wherever I can. Feminist theory also taught me to reconsider my own gender in relation to my body, and learn to inhabit the confusion and uncertainty I find there. I am a man. I am fine calling myself that: the word is not the thing, in any case. I am sexed, yes, but I also know that this aspect of who I am is only considered so significant because I live in a society which is already gendered, and so politically prioritises such a division, and rewards its upkeep, and punishes those already subjected to the violent erasures and brute reductivism of this peculiar obsession with this one kind of difference, in the face of all others.

Most of the time my sex and gender feel like colleagues from different departments, passing each other in a corridor, vaguely aware of each other's business in the same institution. I say most of the time, because the relationship is never static; it depends on what I am doing. I spend so much time inside my head that my body is like the piece of furniture the television sits on. I prefer the days when I don't have to notice it. I know I am lucky to have that option. Perhaps the man that I am is not a gender or a sex, but a diplomat or weary envoy, sent back and forth to broker the terms between contested territories. I carry a sentimental or courteous sense of obligation to abide by the customs and traditions of both, but I don't know if I am obliged more to myself or to others. And now I am this thing called a father, which seems both preposterous and utterly true. True when I think of you. But somehow not when I think of the word, like a clubhouse.

*

A girl. We were asked if we wanted to know at the second scan. We did, and I was so pleased. Selfishly, clumsily from that side of the horizon, I imagined fatherhood as a possibility to indulge in my own gender play. I told myself, If she wants me to plait her hair I will learn to plait her hair. Maybe we can figure out a dance routine one afternoon, or draw faces for each other to name. I saw myself teaching you riffs on my guitar, squinting into the feedback and distortion together, or shaving each other's heads on your sixteenth birthday. *Whatever she wants.* I imagined raising a daughter would see my masculinity neutralised somehow, as if your magnetic charge might finally cancel out my own, and we would meet each other within that neutrality as ourselves. I saw myself in you, or something like that. It's hard to convey. I was wrong about it anyway.

I know that part of me was pleased because I feared having a son. I knew that I would be a resistant companion in masculinity, jaded by its demands in spite of its privileges. And I know the pressures that await a boy more intimately, the ideals against which you are set up to fail, and the punishment and self-hatred when inevitably you do. I never wanted any of it, really. I wonder if any of us did. Growing up, I treasured the people with whom I found respite, and together we endured the passive-aggressive banter, barbed debate and refutation, huffing and spitting, the forced participation in the power plays and dick jokes underwritten with a casual appetite for annihilation, our own if not each other's. Life with the timbre of a football chant, all that posturing and confident noise just to drown out the fear, the fear of being afraid.

Rooms full of men *are* filled with fear, I'm prepared to wager that, though many would deny it. I'm not remotely macho. I expend little effort on the pretence. With other men I tend to deflect, self-deprecate, clown myself into harmless shapes in the hope that my benign appearance defuses any want or need for confrontation. Men fight one another every day – to the death, every day – and knowledge of that fact is a subtextual feature of our daily interactions. This is the absurd yet enduring alpha-male fantasy of hetero-patriarchy. Even though most of us would never challenge another to mortal combat, it remains a vague option out there in the world, and all our banter and debate can feel like codified variants of that same violent potential, like rutting, butting, wrestling towards a state of dominance or submission.

I know that my class, and my whiteness, have afforded me more pathways and easier access to cultural spaces where I do not have to perform a strictly normative version of my gender. I can soften, blur and bend myself and still be listened to, liked, remunerated or promoted. I have little need to worry about coming to physical harm because of how someone reads the relatively soft way I present myself. I am pretty comfortable with being emasculated, because I do not think masculinity is anything to be proud of, and I find its toxic forms repellent. But I know such comfort is a privilege. If we had a son I could only be a patron of vulnerability, and I feared how that might play out for him.

I'm not saying masculinity is the harder path. I know that's not true. The fear of being afraid that we cisgender, heterosexual men carry inside ourselves is most commonly and violently redirected at those who are not cis, heterosexual men. This was also part of my fear of being father to a son: what if, in spite of all my love and gentleness, my son grew up to be aggressive, misogynistic, cold, uncaring? What if I raised a rapist? I mean, fucking hell, that's an awful thing to put onto an as yet unsexed foetus, let alone to write, or say out loud, but it was a thought that stuck, because how can you insure the future against it? Boys can be so dangerous. I don't pretend to know the difficulty of being a woman in the world. Not for a second. And yet, *a girl.* I admit I was relieved.

And now here you are, my daughter, and I have lost the fear of having a son. You have cured me. With hope. You have given me so much hope. You are already far braver than I could ever be on your behalf, and I have realised how far I underestimated a child's dynamism, and how a parent has little choice but to learn to trust a child to become themselves, and that such trust is a kind of love. Children arrive already happening. A son might want his hair plaiting, might want dance routines and distortion irrespective of encouragement or fear. That son might even be you. Your future is not mine to demand or resist and I will learn to live with that uncertainty; I will love you that way.

*

I'm nine or ten years old. I'm in a French church. We're on a family holiday, a boiling August, and we've come inside to escape the midday heat. The air is thick and cool with damp, and has the stillness of a cave. French churches are more interesting than the English churches I've been inside. I don't believe in God, and we only go to church when we visit my grandparents. I sometimes pray, solemnly, but God is only the blackness I see when my eyes are shut, which represents everything that is not me. I don't know how it works. I've never once heard a reply. Above the door a forlorn Jesus looks down from his cross. We've let Him down, we've let His Father down, but most of all we've let ourselves down. In an alcove above the pulpit, Mother Mary appeals heavenwards on our behalf.

St Joan is in the corner, on the left side of the church. She stands there, life-size, or rather my-size, holding her banner. Her sword is cool, her armour realistic. Her expression is pained, but defiant. She is so beautiful. I look at her. And look at her. A girl in armour. I want to be ... I know that at some stage I will grow into a man, but the reality of manhood feels as faint to me as bubbles gathering on the side of a glass. My brother, three years older, is already bristling with a new embarrassment, and a need, at times, to be taken seriously. I keep hearing this word, 'puberty', and some troubling details, but I can't imagine it happening to me, and since I am the youngest in our family no one seems to want it to with any great urgency. Instead, my clowning, my silliness and sensitivity are indulged. I am scruffy and disorganised. I often disappear so thoroughly into my own imagination that I cannot be summoned back by the calling of my name, even after four or five attempts. I try to avoid games where winning and losing are involved. I prefer the company of girls. I just want people to like me. My gender feels like something happening with an increasing external pressure, but, finding no way to either resist or embrace it, I occupy a precarious position, not as a young man, but as a weird mascot.

*

On the day you were born, after those long and blurry first few hours at the hospital, I returned home at around 11 p.m. to change my clothes and get something to eat. I got to the door of the Chinese takeaway just as it was closing, but I told them I had just become a father, and they made me some special fried rice. I got home, ate, fed the oblivious cat, leant my head against the wall of the hallway in our silent flat and I willed it all upon me ... the blood and guts of life. I vowed to look after you as best I could. A solemn vow to undertake the endless work of the present, because I knew that you would occupy it just as much as me, now.

> But could not hide
> My quickening inner life from those at watch.
> They saw a light at a window now and then,
> They had not set there. Who had set it there?

– Elizabeth Barrett Browning

Your inner life has not stopped quickening. It is so radical. I sit and listen as you tell me, between spoonfuls of porridge, your new story, about a girl who became best friends with lava. Who had set it there?

*

In his *Lectures on Physics*, Richard Feynman says that

> when we look for a certain phenomenon we cannot help but disturb it in a certain minimum way, and the disturbance is necessary for the consistency of the viewpoint.

Feynman is talking about the quantum world of particles and atoms. He adds:

> Things on a very small scale behave like nothing that you have any direct experience about. They do not behave like waves, they do not behave like particles, they do not behave like clouds, or billiard balls, or weights on springs, or like anything that you have ever seen.

Quantum mechanics is, in his words, 'the description of the behaviour of matter and light in all its details and, in particular, of the happenings on an atomic scale'. The huge body of theories and processes and equations that emerged throughout the 1920s completely replaced the Newtonian description of the workings of our world: a total revolution. Quantum mechanics remains by far the most successful model for describing the minutiae of nature, with its effectiveness demonstrated by countless experiments. It is of particular interest to me, because poetic thinking is intrinsic to its story and its processes, and, like poetry, it fundamentally accepts uncertainty as a feature of how its knowledge is formed and articulated.

*

When we read a poem, 'we cannot help but disturb it in a certain minimum way', because it requires our imagination to summon it into existence: our disturbance is necessary. Our disturbance is also *our* disturbance uniquely, calling upon our personal experiences and associations in order to imagine a poem into life. This is what makes one's relationship with a poem so intimate, and why a poem disturbs us uniquely in return, as it leaves us variously altered by the time we have each spent with it.

But if we each disturb the poem in our own 'certain minimum way', and are ourselves disturbed by it with each new reading, how can it be the same poem every time? Yet there it is, on the page, the letters and words in their order, the white space around and within them. How can we view a poem as something consistent and know that its existence depends upon the disturbance of our endless multiple readings? We say, *The disturbance is necessary for the consistency of the viewpoint.* We say, The poem is consistently all of the potential readings, and/or it is none of them. We say, A poem does not always exist, but is materialised into a specific place by our interaction with it, by our disturbance.

*

All last week you insisted that you needed a tiara. Your mother sewed one for you, and you treasure it, crying sometimes when you realise that you are not wearing it. Once it's affixed, you return to your game of covertly throwing stones into the fish pond or shouting songs like a brute from your rope swing. You say you are 'a girl', and this seems important to you in that moment, but this is partly because it distinguishes you, 'a big girl', from younger children, from 'babies', and in your mind I can be a girl too, and you frequently invite me to join you in girlhood, without any demand on me to adapt my behaviour. When I agree to be a girl you see no failure in my performance. Girlhood is an inconsistent stylistic inflection upon the wider activity of becoming yourself, becoming a person, and it is that personhood that you pursue most fiercely, every act and gesture bubbling from your crucible. Whatever girlhood is to you, it remains one game among many, a vague shape or idea as far off as Brazil or money, and so you find it pliable, droppable, a means to yourself, a coordinate, but not a destination.

*

Werner Heisenberg was among the first theoretical physicists to describe reality on a quantum scale. He imagined that the tiny electrons that orbit the nuclei of atoms do not always have a fixed location, but *materialise* in a specific place as a result of their interaction with other phenomena. Without these interactions, it is impossible to know with any certainty where an electron is, even if it is possible to use a formula called the Schrödinger equation to predict the probability of where an electron will appear. This might seem insignificant in practical terms, given that the probability value can be predicted with enough accuracy that it enables us to build computers, and rocket ships, and nuclear power stations. But look closely, and the ramifications are clear: a probability is not a certainty, not a promise, it's still a wager, and more than this, the theory that creates the probability value only works because the value is only probable, not *certain* but *uncertain*. As Feynman observes:

We can only predict the odds! This would mean, if it were true, that physics has given up on the problem of trying to predict exactly what will happen in a definite circumstance.

Quantum mechanics is a highly effective interpretation of reality, but not a definition of it, and in order to make its interpretations it retains uncertainty as a fundamental:

> Yes! physics *has* given up. *We do not know how to predict what would happen in a given circumstance*, and we believe now that it is impossible, that the only thing that can be predicted is the probability of different events.

For a poet, this is a familiar principle. We have given up trying to predict what will happen to our poems in a definite circumstance. Yesterday, I wrote:

> If you are unsure
> what you want from life, and include me
> in that confusion, I can still offer water,
> or else go back downstairs to sit and stir,
> on your behalf, this brilliant white emulsion.

Do I know what that 'brilliant white emulsion' means in a definite way? To myself, or to you, or to anyone? Not with any certainty. But I offer it, having calculated a probability value.

Trusting a reader to follow you when you make such leaps is a risk, and one that poets take and weigh in their work to various degrees. But that trust is, I think, a fundamental of poetic language too: it is our uncertainty principle. Describing the world on a poetic scale that includes both the minutiae and expansiveness of sensorial and psychological experience, also requires more than classical laws and arithmetic, and so poets must also risk our 'only probable' calculations.

But the uncertainty principle of poetry is not unique. All languages are poetic, in a sense. Poetry is a context, a kind of framing that places uncertainty in the foreground, but even words stored within the highly controlled environment of the dictionary require interaction with the words around them to materialise in their probable, calculable place. A word has no intrinsic, permanent quality; in order for a word to appear to us as a defined, particular unit of meaning, it must reveal itself via its interplay with other terms, and in a context of renewal and exchange which is no less of a wager. Etymology is the fossil record or DNA code, not the living creature.

*

'Saint Joan of Arc' did not live or die as a saint, or even as a Joan.

She did not come from a place called 'Arc'.

Jehanne was known, growing up, by her nickname, Jehannette.

It is important to remember that a real woman was burned alive.

Her father, a farmer, was from Arc, but Jehanne never went there herself.

Jehanne Romée, the real woman, who was burned alive, was born in Domrémy, where daughters took their mothers' names if they took a surname at all.

Someone on her mother's side had once been to Rome as a pilgrim, and so returned to find the surname 'Romée' waiting for them, just as it was waiting for Jehanne when she was born in Domrémy.

During her trial Jehanne referred to herself only as 'la Pucelle', the maid.

Her maidenhead was a fact that both the French physicians of the dauphin, her future king, and the English physicians took pains to establish. A real woman endured these inspections.

45

Jehanne was put on trial even though the evidence against her was insufficient under inquisitorial rules and the bishop leading the proceedings lacked jurisdiction under ecclesiastical law.

The tribunal court itself was packed with English and Burgundian clerics, and members of the French clergy were denied a seat in proceedings.

The articles of accusation that the court subsequently levelled at Jehanne were different from those in the court's own record, portions of which, it was later admitted, had already been doctored in her disfavour.

In order to make Jehanne's heresy a capital crime, the court had to prove her a repeat offender. For this they used the fact of Jehanne's cross-dressing, including during her time in prison, where she only continued to wear men's clothes to protect herself from rape.

Under inquisitorial law a Jehanne should have been held in an ecclesiastical prison, guarded not by soldiers but by nuns.

Jehanne was burned alive in public. Who is Joan of Arc?

*

Isn't all knowledge underpinned by an uncertainty principle? Everything I know is only *as far as I know*. Probable. To be certain would be to consider knowledge finished, to accept that I can know no further. Knowledge is something ongoing, upheld by the processes of its continual reapplication. Its effectiveness and validity is always undergoing the test of its truthfulness. What we know includes the uncertainty implicit in the burden of its proof. How wrong-headed to think of uncertainty as a weaker position, or as an impasse, when uncertainty is so clearly a positive cognitive stance. It invites ingenuity, curiosity, and includes within its caveat the possibility of new knowledge. It gives the known a future. Without uncertainty knowledge-making would grind to a halt. New knowledge must surely arise out of acts of epistemic disobedience and playfulness, not from knowing what we know already.

*

Take for example the German physicist Max Planck. In 1900, he was conducting a thought experiment exploring how objects radiate heat, a common area of interest for physicists at that time. All objects with a temperature above absolute zero emit electromagnetic radiation across a wide spectrum of wavelengths. What we call 'visible light' just refers to the radiation that falls within the narrow part of that spectrum that our eyes can actually detect. The different wavelengths of that radiation can be seen by us, correspondingly, as different colours.

For a hotter object, more of the energy will be radiated at shorter wavelengths. The interior of a toaster, for example, contains filaments which emit radiation that peaks within the orangey-red part of the visual spectrum, but hotter objects emit more of the even-shorter wavelengths of radiation, which appear blue and green. The shortest range of radiation wavelengths that we can see appear a violet colour, corresponding to a temperature of around 15,000 degrees Celsius. Shorter still, and we move outside of the visual range to ultraviolet wavelengths of radiation, then X-rays, and, shortest of all, gamma rays. Any object emitting these would be extremely, extremely hot.

To explore this phenomenon, physicists have conceived of an idealised object called a black body, which absorbs radiation at all frequencies and reflects none. With reflection taken out of the equation, they can be sure that all radiation emanating from the black body comes from within. This means that physicists are able to accurately measure the wavelengths of energy radiated. A black body can be theorised as any object with perfect emissivity, or can be approximated in reality for the purposes of experiment, by cutting a small hole in the door of an oven, for instance,

47

which would allow for the emission of radiation from the black body without upsetting the thermal equilibrium of the body itself. The radiation a black body emits thus depends only on its temperature, not on its make-up, and for the sake of the theory physicists assume that its temperature is constant and uniform.

The relationship between the temperature and the distribution of the radiation wavelengths, however, remained a mystery at the time that Planck conducted his own investigation.

Planck, standing on the edge of what was known, and with a little disobedient playfulness, decided to describe black body radiation mathematically, not in terms of a continuous spectrum of wavelengths, but as discrete units, imagining that the energy was not wave-like in nature but distributed somehow in finite packets, blocks, 'quanta'. It was, in his own words, 'purely a formal assumption and I really did not give it much thought'. 'Formal', that is, in the sense that he had no idea about the physical reality; but the playful, mathematical procedure was soon proved right in countless experiments.

It was Einstein who, five years later, claimed that Planck's quanta were not just a mathematical trick, but real, physical things, 'a finite number of energy quanta which are localised at points in space, which move without dividing, and which can only be produced and absorbed as complete units'. Photons. And so followed the next hundred and twenty years of quantum theory and particle physics, a total revolution in our understanding of the world around us, with unfathomable practical applications: smartphones, computers, atomic clocks, transistors, LEDs, fibre-optic cables, MRI scanners, and many other innovations and processes in medicine and chemistry. All are modern descendants of Planck's playful mathematical assumption: energy in packets. These ideas are still unravelling a century later, are still at play.

*

It is impossible [. . .] for any poet, while he is writing a poem, to observe with complete accuracy what is going on, to define with any certainty how much of the final result is due to subconscious activity over which he has no control, and how much is due to conscious artifice.

– W. H. Auden

*

Consider light. Light has classically been shown to behave like a wave, but we know that it is comprised of particles: the packets of energy that Planck calculated and Einstein theorised as photons.

In the famous 'double slit' experiment, a light source is positioned next to a screen with two slits in it. The light arrives at the screen like a wave.

The light then reaches the screen and passes through the two slits, creating two new waves, which interfere with one another as they overlap, spreading out.

These waves then hit a second screen, where we can register the interference of the waves: peaks where the two waves have amplified one another, and troughs where they have cancelled each other out. Classic wave-like behaviour. This is how light has been recorded, observed and thought about since the early nineteenth century.

However, the arrival of Einstein's photons meant that physicists had to rethink the nature of light as now being comprised of individual units of electromagnetic radiation, like tiny balls of light energy. Imagine you were to fire a bucket of ball bearings at a screen with two slits in it: they would simply pass through whichever slit they arrived at and proceed to the second screen in a straight line without overlapping or spreading out. And yet photons, when fired through the double slits, still organise themselves in such a way that they create the wave-like interference pattern on the second wall. The behaviour of the photon presents itself as a contradiction to us, because we do not encounter anything behaving like it in the world. Our mind has not evolved to compute the existence of wave-particles because we never encounter them with our senses. So our conceptual metaphors are not good enough to reconcile the behaviour of wave and ball bearing.

Maybe somehow the photons are knocking into one another? Maybe they influence each other according to some undetectable force? The problem is, if you slow things down and try to examine the phenomenon by firing individual light photons one ball bearing at a time, the photons still create the interference pattern; fired individually, they still end up at the second screen distributed as if they had arrived there as a wave. Each ball bearing is a wave unto itself.

Then, in a further diversion from reality on the scale that we encounter it, when you set up a detection apparatus to find out which of the slits each individual photon goes through, the wave pattern completely disappears. It's as if the photons know they are being watched, and decide to stop behaving like a wave and instead behave like ball bearings. And then, when you turn off the detection apparatus, the ball bearings start creating the wave pattern again. What can we conclude? Does light behave like a wave or a particle? Feynman writes that 'it really behaves like neither. Now we have given up. We say: "It is like *neither*."' Light is not behaving strangely; our minds are simply limited in their imaginative scope.

*

The light comes in the name of the voice. [. . .] I am not bound to answer you.

— Jehanne Romée, from the transcript of her trial, 1431

*

Experiment 1: Wave-Particle Duality As a Metaphor for Metaphor

'The sun is a blood orange':
the sentence arrives like a wave, there is
an interference pattern within it:
the sentence interferes within itself,
the blood-orange-sun arriving.

The sun is a blood orange.
It looked heavy as it set, its colour
bleeding out into the sky, I said
'The sun is a blood orange'.
Nothing mysterious about that.

Each day we encounter with our senses
an interference pattern.

51

But this is not consistent with the theory
of a 'word-particle'.

The theory says, Words are discrete units,
they leave and arrive with us
as packets, chunks and lumps, as quanta,
localised, the word 'sun' or 'orange'
at a point in space.

How can the local 'sun'
also be a 'blood orange'?
How can a 'blood orange' then
also be 'the sun'?

We have given up.
We say, Wave-particle-word duality.
We say, When we look for the word
we cannot help but disturb it
in a certain minimum way
and the disturbance is necessary
for the consistency of the sentence
bleeding into the sky, even now,
with the consistency of blood
but the taste and the weight
and the shape of a colour
in the sky in my hand.

*

If I cannot be a man, perhaps I can be a kind of Joan. This real-isation happens thoughtlessly, wordlessly; it was already there. Mum is calling to me in the silent church in a stage whisper. It is time to go, back to the market, the hot car. I look up at Joan a final time, and I take a deep breath. I tell myself, If I can hold it until I get outside Joan will ... Will what? Protect me? Love me? I don't know. But I hold my breath back through the church, round past the font and out through the doors, where the day is a bright, white rectangle, a portal I pass through, carrying my new secret into the blaring sunshine.

*

I'm not saying that I 'identified' with Joan. I find that idea uncomfortable. Evoking another historic or mythic figure in place of yourself tends to be mawkish, even as a literary device, and it can also be insensitive to different historical and social contexts and privileges. I've struggled with that in my own poems, and have found that in any case you only really evoke another part of yourself when you call upon other people to do your talking; every translator is stuck on their side of the mirror.

Joan of Arc is remarkable because of her seemingly endless evocability. Even in her lifetime, Jehanne was read symbolically, an embodied metonym of conflicting secular claims: on righteousness, on land and law. A holy icon and heretic iconoclast, a warrior and a maid, a figure of both fear and inspiration, later adopted as a heroine by far-right nationalists, suffragettes, feminists, secular poets, presbyters and priests. Joan is not a contradiction, she is a wave-particle. She is duality and she is neither.

And Joan's duality and neitherness allowed me to stand at the edge of what I knew. Her image helped me to materialise, fixed me into position, but also allowed me to retain all my patterns of interference. But I know that, wave after particle after wave, Joan's neitherness belongs to no one.

*

Pushing you in the buggy down in town, people treat me differently. They smile and hold doors open. Men soften their expressions, make space for me on the pavement, stepping into the road. Women find my presence benign. I feel genderless and round, a goodly whale, meaning no harm. In the café an old woman leans into the buggy where you sit beneath your orange bobble hat. The woman smiles, then, looking up at me, asks, *How old is your son?*

*

Experiment 2: Wave-Particle Duality and the Changing Interference Patterns of a Child Practising Itself

We shall now try the following experiment . . .

To our [child] . . . we add a very strong light source

You are taking instruction, but from where?

. . . from both places at the same time

We must conclude that *when we look*
. . . *the* [child] . . . is different
than when we do not look.

. . . there is an element of assessment to the way
you observe yourself

. . . our light source . . . disturbs things . . .

You say you are 'a girl', and this seems important
to you in that moment

It must be . . . very delicate,
when it scatters . . . gives the . . . [child]
a jolt that changes their motion.

... a cruelty towards oneself that no amount
of practice can alleviate

                              ... So perhaps we *should* expect the motion
                                                        to be changed.

... it might help you retain the full futurity
of your personhood

                              Anyway ... the light exerts
                              a big influence on the [child].

It feels creepy, and like an attack on your future
                              That is, the jolt ...
                              You may be thinking: 'Don't ...!

Turn the brightness down! The light ... weaker and ... not
    disturb ... so much. It may be a ... way to avoid it.

                              Is there not *some* way ...
                              without disturbing them?

                              ... What is the machinery behind the law?'

... this peculiar obsession with this one kind
of difference, in the face of all others

              No one has found any machinery behind the law.

                              ... This is all a little discouraging.

                                                          ... but ...

Maybe we can figure out a dance routine

                              'Perhaps the [child] has ... internal works
                                          some inner variables
                                    ... we do not ... know
                                    ... we ... limit ourselves ...
                              We say 'at the present time' ... for ever

                                          ... it is impossible ...

                                    ... this is the way nature really *is*.

... such trust is a kind of love

            When a [child] can occur in several alternative ways.

IV.

THE LANGUAGE OF MATHEMATICS AND A FUNERAL FOR THE KNOWN

Is it dead?
Yes.
Can I see it?
Yes.

I hold out the body of the mouse on the dustpan. You look at it with an expression on your face somewhere between fascination, revulsion and fear, which quickly softens into something . . . quieter. You look up at me with a question in your mind, but you don't know how to ask it. I smile back at you, reassuringly, just to say 'don't worry', and you return a nervous smile of your own. Maybe I'm kidding. About the mouse. About it being dead. Or maybe my smile means *We are still alive.*

*

I remember lying awake in my room as a child, listening to the burbling of the television downstairs, and the muffled vowel-sounds of my parents talking, the sense of an adult evening-world taking place without me. I don't know how I came to be thinking about death and what it might be like to be dead, I just remember the process of subtraction I enacted in my mind while trying to imagine it.

Death would be soundless   [I blocked my ears]

Death would be darkness   [I shut my eyes]

And I wouldn't be breathing   [I held my breath]

Each time I tried to create the conditions of being dead, my living body would ruin it: when I shut my eyes there were these annoying drifting fluorescent specks, when I blocked up my ears there remained a low, constant rumbling; I could hold my breath, but I could feel myself holding it, and I couldn't stop my heart from thumping, or my thoughts from spooling ... Eventually something caught and turned over – *I* could not create the conditions of death because, for *that*, *I* would need to not be here. It was as if my brain had run beyond the floor beneath it, and was madly treading air. I tried again to find a thought, to tether the realisation in language, but no terms arrived. In the dark, in my room, death became a singularity.

I howled in panic. Dad came up. *I don't want to die!* I pleaded. He put his arms around me, and his heat and his body were more like a place than a person. *Hey, hey,* he said, *What are you worrying about that for? You're not going to die.* And then I remember there was a pause, during which time his mind must have redacted that shred of a lie, and instead traced the trajectory of my thoughts back to the truth: that one day I would be gone from the world and my world would be gone. It must have caught, turned over and shuddered across him too, because he added, *not for a long time*, quietly, to reassure us both.

A childhood neighbour once told my parents how she used to

watch me ride my bike down the hill beside our house and throw myself into the bushes at the bottom, arranging myself dead and prone, lying there for minutes at a time. Eventually I would get up, take my bike to the top of the hill and do the whole thing over again. I did this regularly, she said. I remember doing it too, though not what I sought by doing it. Nor why I did it so repeatedly, as if rehearsing.

*

Before you were born I used to imagine my funeral pretty regularly. I'd be washing up, a song would come on the cheesy radio station I used to listen to and I'd feel ... *lifey*, nostalgic for the present, and my mind would wander, out of perverse habit, to a church, or whatever, filling with faceless mourners. I am dead and the person I was is being weighed there with a finality that I will never know in life, no matter how much I might crave it. Indulgent? Narcissistic? Yes, totally. That's allowed in one's own head. The whole fantasy is so indistinct and vague, that I know I'm not actually trying to imagine what my funeral will be like, but instead trying to locate something reassuringly fixed or whole about myself, to diffuse the anxiety of experiencing life as ongoing and uncertain and disparate. I make this idle, romantic plea to my imagination to know who I am.

I don't do that much any more. I don't fear and obsess about my own death in the way I used to before you were born. It seems obvious to me that this is because my death has been superseded by a greater fear, or cluster of fears, that I hardly dare to form in my mind, let alone put into words.

*

When you were a newborn, we were told that, like with all newborns, there was a small chance you might stop breathing. Most likely this would happen when you were asleep. For no known or particular medical reason. We were given advice and a number of recommendations based on the statistical evidence gathered from past circumstances of sudden infant death syndrome, but we were also told that even if we followed every recommendation, it could still happen anyway. The only reassurance was that it probably wouldn't, which of course is no reassurance at all.

I have never recovered from that fear. It fucked me up. Irreparably. At first, I found it impossible to go to sleep. Listening to you breathing and breathing, I would drift in that awful, tense, vigilant state, then, checking my phone, I'd find I'd entered another hour. When I did sleep, it came so fast, was so heavy and dreamless that I would wake with a start, to a quiet room, panic heaving through my chest, like a wave raking shingle from the beach. Holding it and holding it, until finally I found you, your breath so soft and quiet, I could only discern it by the barely audible movement of your blanket rising and falling. Relief, my favourite emotion. The wave breaking.

Because I couldn't trust you to stay alive, and I could not stay awake for ever, there was nothing else to do but say *so be it* and force my face onto the pillow. It felt like leaving you outside the city walls, like wading down into the reeds to float you off downstream. I grieved. I grieved for you, but also at the realisation that my whole life now would be bent to this task of giving you away, offering you up from our life and into the widening jaws of your own. *What a cruel fucking trick!* If I had not been so exhausted and anxious I would have raged, and sobbed.

I am learning to live within the fear; it is huge, architectural, orchestral, my fear for you. I have been flooded with new histamines, and although my mind and my body are only very limited tools for your care and protection, I have pledged them entirely to that function.

For months and months I was so catastrophic and alert to threats, which were largely the invention of my own dark imagination, that I was quite happy to wake at two-hour intervals. It was an excuse to check on you, to lift you close and carry you to your mother, who fed you while I sat beside her, calling her name softly if she started dropping off. When you started sleeping through, I found myself waiting in the dark, anticipating a cry, or else I shuffled about the rooms of the night, both the rooms in my head and those in our flat. I was furious with myself for not being able to stop the unspooling, to stop myself gnawing and grating the compacted terror at the base of my skull. But now I am a veteran. I know when I need to get up, know to ignore my phone and try and read poems by lamplight, the more obscure the better. I know when a panic attack is coming, like the drop in air pressure ahead of a downpour. I have been to the doctor and pleaded with him to cure me of my numerous incurable phantom diseases. I have begged myself to cry, for a release from the stress of it, and found only a feeling that I am falling forwards. I have brokered a deal with my reflection in the kitchen window at night, to try and be happier, and saluted myself with another glass of cold December water from the tap. I really had myself worried, for a while, back there.

I'm reconciled to the fear of love. It is so strange how readily expendable I feel. Not the same as wanting to die, but a total willingness to die should the need arise. I am ready to plunge my hand into the whirring machinery, to gulp the poison down, take it safely inside. Other fathers told me about a hyper-protective instinct they discovered, a bristling new aggression and primed attentiveness to whatever threat might enter the mouth of the cave, but I have never really felt or conceived of this threat as material, snarling and prehistoric, or lurking behind a hedge near the swings. I've just experienced a shift in my personhood, and acquired this sense of my body as happy collateral, a buffer of meat. I'm not the important one in my life any more. That old romance has faded. I remember it like the interior of a bedroom in a previous house.

*

Funerals are not to do with death, or dying, at least not the ones I have been to; funerals belong to the living, since the dead do not attend, not really. At the end of a life we try to weigh it, see it, know the person more wholly in their absence. It is the absence of the deceased that sets the mourners into motion, as they talk and move and think *about* the dead person, who now only exists between them. I think about Reinhard Genzel and his team, whether they could chart the movement of mourners, drawn *about* that absent centre. Maybe that's what a funeral is: a way of describing and charting the departed by such coalescences, now that we cannot reach them or encounter them directly with our senses.

I have often been struck by the way that funerals bring together a fuller spectrum of people to one place than tends to happen in life: work colleagues weeping alongside childhood friends and family; a new neighbour passing an order of service along to an incognito ex-lover. We perform ourselves so differently to the different people in our lives, and yet at our funerals there they all are, our panel, our audience, our conference. It is an unrealistic portrait on account of its holism; in life we are rarely so broadly triangulated. But the description given of the deceased by the ceremonial language of the funeral, with its pressurisation of emotion into slow, ordered increments, like a kind of grammar, nevertheless affords a rare and distinct articulacy: we might not have been all the versions of ourselves known to the people we knew *all at once*, but we were still all those versions. And isn't that a more honest appraisal of what our personhood is, than the one that sees us as consistent, reduced to a median or mean?

The ceremonial language of the funeral is also articulate

because of all the particular animate bodies gathering in relation to the singular inanimacy of the dead body, its gravity having drawn us there, as if grief were responsible for a curvature in space and time, which in my experience it is. At funerals we see how much we are made between each other. We are reminded of the magnitude of our connectedness, our physical presence in one another's lives. It never stops, the touching, the meeting, the endless chancy business of our encounters, the versions of each other that we carry around, even after death. The language of the funeral describes life precisely in those terms, as we gather, to declare by our gathering, how we verify and give life to each other.

To imagine your own funeral is to try and locate something of your own singularity, your source of gravity. You are asking what force your life enacts on others. If you became a massive absence, who would be drawn into its orbit?

*

In her brilliant and illuminating book *What Can She Know?*, feminist philosopher Lorraine Code examines the role that subjectivity plays in the making of knowledge claims. First she highlights how within the western philosophical tradition 'a demonstrable alignment between the ideals of autonomous reason and ideals of masculinity' has led to the systemic removal of the figure of knower from the known. Code writes that

> the ideals of masculinity that align with ideals of reason derive – locally, specifically – from the experiences of the men who construct the dominant theories of both.

These men have, over the centuries, been guided by the idealistic belief that knowledge worthy of the name is timelessly and placelessly true, and that its objects are disconnected from knowing subjects [. . .] and unaffected by the knowing process.

How can knowledge be 'timelessly and placelessly true'? Where does it stand, like an obelisk, disembodied, permanent and universal? Isn't knowledge precisely reliant on the fact that somebody knows it? Code continues:

Theorists who adhere to this 'autonomy of knowledge' persuasion maintain that knowledge properly so-called transcends experience, whose particularity can only sully and muddle its purity and clarity. [. . .] Where there are no universal standards, the argument goes, there can be no knowledge worthy of the name.

You can see the slippery slope implied by such reasoning: the moment you acknowledge the role and presence of the knower in the known, everything becomes subjective, personal, and we tumble into the impasse of relativism: our precious facts disappear. But if the very idea of autonomous knowledge relies on an idealisation of data – as information existing separate from both the processes that apprehend and create it and the minds that read and interpret it – what kind of truth is being upheld? This fantasy of knowledge, purified and cleaned of all its human elements, does not belong to reality. It is a fetish object, and, ironically, one that only exists in the human imagination which desires and guards its possibility. It is a deeply religious commitment to reason, underpinned by the absolute denial of the very cognitive mechanisms that might prove such truths to be true.

Code offers a correction. She writes that 'understanding the circumstances of the knower [actually] makes possible a more *discerning* evaluation'. Erasing ourselves from the process of knowing is not merely bad philosophical practice, but it represents a threat to the variety and vitality of the different kinds of knowledge that we live our lives by. In doing so, Code also reintroduces us to the inequity and injustices evident in the way that knowledge-forms are policed and sociopolitically prioritised. She invites us to confront the reality of the oppression suffered by groups of different knowers, and to consider how their knowledge-claims are neglected, marginalised and erased.

Western philosophy's demand for mythical certainties, for universal 'truths', arises out of the denial of the human processes on which knowledge is founded in the first place. The processes of debate, refutation, experiment and refinement are not eradicated by a final result or agreement, but stand as evidence of knowledge-making as an ephemeral process of becoming and ongoingness. Moreover, the knowledge that we agree upon as 'objectively true' can only be held as such by subjects, and according to specific terms, interpreted to within an acceptable range of accuracy, within and across languages. Far from being autonomous and divorced from the dirty business of human subjectivity, the truth comes about and is kept afloat precisely through a communal process of intersubjective exchange and agreement.

This is one reason why the division in academia between the sciences and humanities is misleading, if not misguided. The humanities, when seen through an idealised 'masculine' lens, can easily be devalued for producing knowledge more visibly dependent on subjective, interpretive claims. Instead of being praised for their adaptability, dynamism, and their dialogic and social potential, the humanities and the knowledge they produce are often positioned as intellectual luxuries. At the same time, the belief that mathematics and science subjects generate autonomously objective knowledge completely misunderstands the creative, uncertain, metaphorical and speculative processes that we can find at their very heart.

'Schemes, practices, and paradigms evolve out of communal projects of inquiry', as Code says, and this is true of all knowledge-forms. Irrespective of our specialism or discipline it is our duty, our great communal and political responsibility, to make these schemes useful, knowable, and true to others. It's our duty as knowers to gather around an uncertainty, and to hold our little funeral for the truth. In doing so we can corral what we know into agreement, pressed by a responsibility to all the knowers who would know.

Poetry seeks this situation of uncertain, collaborative knowledge-making. I go to poems in the hope of having my own confusion about the world clarified according to the confusion of someone else's. That shared confusion is not without benefit or accuracy; I rarely feel closer to another mind than when reading a poem. The burden of knowing on my own is unreasonable, and poems save me from the loneliness of such autonomy. Like the solemn encircling of mourners *about* the life now gone, a poem calls readers together towards a communal articulacy.

*

My lantern is a hopeful lantern.
No cairns on the fairway
but the crosshatch and fish scales
on the backs of our hands
until finally, yes, this item in time,
I see you in it. Don't you agree?
Ideas limbering up on the concourse,
all verby and nouny. Questions gone hot
in our mouths. And the answers?
Whatever's the opposite to a tug of war.

*

66

At school I was quite good at maths, though I found it boring. Each week the class would be taught a new process, a way of unpacking or repacking something, or finding out from one set of values the value of something else, like an angle or a length, or the number that *x* 'stood in' for. We learned to repeat these processes until we could enact them more or less without thinking. The more rote the mechanics of the equations became, the further away from any reality they seemed, abstracting into a game of moves and values of its own. Maths felt like a meta-language that talked back to itself, and whenever an exam question asked us to imagine a process we had learned in a way that corresponded with a real-life situation, it would seem faintly absurd:

> We can say that each cow in the field
> is able to observe 6 sheep and 5 (other) cows.

> We can therefore say, 'Each cow can see
> one more sheep than cows.'

But I remember there being something satisfying about the way that sums and calculations moved, like each joint in a leg bending and adjusting until gradually a step could be taken. And then, with fluency, these became dance steps, elegant and precise. I also liked the idea that the values *x*, *y*, *a* and *d* could stand in for anything as long as the rule of their relation remained consistent. You could be describing the fabric of space, or the lining of your jacket, it didn't seem to matter; as long as you let the equation play out according to its own rules, your cutlery would align.

Perhaps those italicised letters, standing in with their gentle, lean and hand-written character of impermanence, announce their metaphorical potential for mutation, and as a teenager, unsure about my own mutating shape, I identified with them. I know that I understood them as symbolic creatures, that their *standing in* was an efficient version of the way the word 'cow' might *stand in* for a real cow in nature. I learned maths as a meta-language, as something that interrelated perfectly, but that required a certain amount of good faith, if you wanted to reconcile its terminology and descriptions with the things it sought to describe in reality. Maths can brag a certain exactitude in terms of self-reference, according to its theory, but it must be applied, must be held against the world we inhabit and experience, to have meaning.

*

> *One, two, three, four, five, six . . .*
> Good, keep going.

You have been able to count for a while now, though I'm not sure that's true. First come the sounds of the numbers, little clumps of noise to shape with your mouth. You got to ten quickly. But now something has changed; you have begun to assign the sound to an object. The number is a temporary name, and the objects are units to be named.

> *. . . seven, eight . . .*

You put your finger onto each as you go, sometimes skipping over and getting the wrong result, or counting the same thing twice, giving it two temporary names. Now you have the hang of it, counting is a game and you feel pleased when you have counted correctly; the renaming gives you pleasure.

> *. . . nine, ten . . .*
> Well done!

The objects themselves recede, as they become units in the game, or rather the features that distinguish them as singular are lost to the foregrounding of the system. I have noticed you find it easier to count if the objects are similar, as if the difference between the things you are counting goes against the act, causes some contradiction in your mind that you have to work around. And you do work around it, because to do so wins the game and makes you happy.

Very good.
forty, four, eight, seven, four ...

*

In their book *Where Mathematics Comes From*, the linguist George Lakoff and the cognitive scientist Rafael E. Núñez, argue that maths, rather than being an innate feature of the universe, is in fact a very human sort of system, which we invented in order to describe phenomena to ourselves. More than that, they show that maths exhibits many of the same design features of other languages, in that it is conceptually founded on metaphors to do with our physical processes. For example, if our senses were able to apprehend the quantum world – its photons whooshing through our bodies, our bodies emitting light, and all the particles of the world around us being brought into existence only by their collision and interaction – would we have conceived of discrete number units? It seems so natural for us to imagine the world being divided into clumps and chunks because that is how our minds and senses have evolved to find it ... a rock here, a stick there.

Lakoff and Núñez take what's known as a fictionalist, or anti-realist stance. For them maths is a fiction, which humankind has 'made up' according to the specifically evolved limits of the human mind, in order to describe and predict phenomena, even that which we cannot apprehend directly with our senses. On the other side of the debate are those known as realists, who believe that maths is something *real*, something out there, and has always been out there: a Platonic maths, which we 'discover' piece by piece. For Lakoff and Núñez, a belief in such a transcendent maths is unreasonable:

> Platonic mathematics, like God, cannot in itself be perceived or comprehended via the human body, brain, and mind. Science alone can neither prove nor disprove the existence of a Platonic mathematics, just as it cannot prove or disprove the existence of a God.

In order to support the case for fictionalism, Lakoff and Núñez worked with a team of mathematicians to set about examining the metaphorical, cognitive bases that underpin the fundamental mathematical theorems and principles without which maths could not function: arithmetic as motion along a path, sets as containers, continuity in terms of gaplessness, numbers as object collections, etc. They found that

> metaphors are an essential part of mathematical thought, not just auxiliary mechanisms used for visualization or ease of understanding [. . .] a great many of the most fundamental mathematical ideas are inherently metaphorical in nature.

If this is the case, then maths is a language. It is constructed according to the limited physical, comprehensive faculties of the brain as it has specifically evolved; maths is a theoretical description of reality, but it is not part of reality outside of the human mind; its theories can be tested against reality and return effective numerical results with which we might be said to make accurate predictions, but the numerical results with which we describe such accuracies are just as theoretical, part of the same system underpinned by the same cognitive metaphors.

This applies to any language; we can only test a language's accuracy by using more of it, or else in terms of other languages. And since all languages, across all translations, are self-referring systems, we are always speaking and writing at one fundamental remove from the reality we experience. The physicist Carlo Rovelli writes:

> The world is complex, and we capture it with different languages, each appropriate to the process which we are describing. Every complex process can be addressed and understood in different languages and at different levels.

Of course we can refine and diversify our terms to the point of near faultless accuracy, and this is perhaps why mathematics is often believed to transcend the limits of other languages: because it is so effective. In fact, the mathematician Eugene Paul Wigner, has written of 'the unreasonable effectiveness of mathematics in the natural sciences'. His article of the same name discusses how the accuracy of mathematical theory, as proven by experimentation, transcends our understanding of it; mathematics is therefore unreasonable in its effectiveness:

> The miracle of the appropriateness of the language of mathematics for the formulation of the laws of physics is a wonderful gift which we neither understand nor deserve.
>
> – Eugene Paul Wigner

As a poet, I feel envious of mathematicians. But the feeling passes. This is because I am inclined to remember the unreasonable effectiveness of the language I write in. Even now, these thoughts and ideas can be conveyed with a demonstrable accuracy between us, and isn't that unreasonably effective too? Think how much ground we can cover! We forget about the unreasonable effectiveness of our 'everyday' languages because speaking and writing and making gestures are skills that most of us possess; the sentence is a technological advancement no one can remember or imagine living without, or prior to.

And poetry, what is that? Not everyday language, but a specialised one, developed to speak to the mysterious universe outside of the usually defined limits of language itself. Poems have not put man on the moon, but the poetic symbolism of that achievement has probably been its most enduring outcome. Putting a man on the moon was one of our best poems.

*

We speak of mathematics as if it were a Platonic, purely factual, objective system, somehow unrelated to the rest of human life and language, unrelated to the biology of the human brain or the highly particular and limited design of the mind, but, as Lakoff and Núñez have shown, this is not the case. We also tend to forget that mathematics is often taught and expressed through other languages. These other languages have been present at each stage of every technological advance of the last century – debate, discussion, spitballing over coffee – so it is strange that we tend to accredit the huge technological developments of the last century to the advancement and application of mathematical thinking. Typically, the creative imagination has driven innovation: playful experiments both within and outside of the language of maths itself. Most scientists will happily and readily reveal the fundamental uncertainty at the centre of their theorising, modelling and experimentation. Analogy and metaphor are intrinsic to every language. Poetry and its uncertain epistemological stance has been there the whole time.

*

Death, I realised, would be like nothing,
not an obelisk, not a turn in the river
to encounter with our senses, no metaphors
to find it *like for like* in mind, nor can we touch
it with clouds, abstract or italic,
or knowledge, Platonic, autonomous,
unsullied by any knower worth the name,
only that total open-ended opposite,
daughter, don't be scared, or else be scared,
as in 'very alive and so much part of love'.
Death is a romance beyond numbers,
and never *here* at all, but life?

Is a closed system that can only refer
to itself. Unreasonably effective.
And so articulate. Can you feel that?
Everything speaking at once.

*

Two years before you were born your mother and I travelled back
to the village where I grew up, to visit your grandparents and
watch the local firework display. We had just received the news
of a close friend's terminal diagnosis. The fortnight before we had
attended the funeral of another friend who had killed himself.
It felt as if the world was more permeable, as if one thing might
bleed or disappear into the next. I couldn't do my coat up tight
enough. We stood around in the dark, as the crowd gathered:
people I recognised from the village, my old neighbours, faces I
remembered vaguely from school, now adults. Then my brother
(your uncle) and his wife (your auntie) arrived, with your two
cousins, and we chatted, and I asked the boys questions about
their ear protectors, and wellington boots when all of a sudden
the firework display started, and everyone looked up together.

73

People moved into lines to stand watch as the great argument played out above us. Each of us stood on our unique little spot on the earth, and without saying or doing anything we declared ourselves and our unfathomable relation to one another. It was a funeral and a poem, looking up at the same thing; the unreasonable effectiveness of the language of life in describing itself, 'without any irritable reaching after fact and reason'.

V.

A GIRL IN ARMOUR DREAMS OF LIVING FOR EVER

What are you laughing at?
I'm just laughing at this message from Emily.
From Emily?
I'm reading a message on my phone that she sent me.
Can I see?
Sure.
Where is she? Where is Emily?

You have grown up surrounded by technology that can summon people into the room, their voices into the air, their faces onto a screen. Growing up, we only had a landline plugged in at the wall and a portable television. The phone was a chunky, dense, red, plastic apparatus, with a receiver that sat on top like the horns of a water buffalo. You had to ring the numbers round on a dial, which would slide back to the starting position with a satisfying sound. The convention at that time was to pick up and answer by saying your phone number. By the time I was allowed to use the phone I already knew the number by heart, because I had heard my parents intone it hundreds of times.

Maybe it's even possible that I knew our phone number before I could count to ten, I don't know. Typically, I am not nostalgic (I find nostalgia compresses and reduces experiences into a romantic wad, which is also the opposite of poetry to me, which retains complication and keeps the particular in play) but I allow myself a little sentimentality about those numbers in a line, because they were, for a long time, like the song of our house and I can summon my parents' voices so clearly by them. Now, when I call your grandparents up, they just pick up and say 'Hello' like a question, which saddens a small corner of me, even though I teased them for keeping up the earlier habit some years into the new millennium.

The technology of my childhood had seams. You knew you were using it. But you will grow up in a world where the interface is so intuitive that your portals can appear with a gesture no less natural to you than picking up a cup, or scratching your nose. When my dad first got an iPad he told me that one morning he caught himself trying to zoom in on the paper surface of his newspaper, un-pinching his thumb and middle finger on the page. By the time I am his age, that might even be possible, though it seems more likely that news will arrive in a fashion we can't even conceive of yet ... without a thought, a word, a gesture in the air ...

We try to limit your screen time, though I dearly love watching television, especially with you, so I can't be too much of a hypocrite. I watched as much television as I could as a child and never found that it encouraged passivity of thought. If anything, it inspired fantasies of my own, gave me imaginative prompts and points of departure to then extend in play. It brought me the wonders of the world and beyond: armadillos, space rockets, talking cars, French kissing, the news. I don't worry about your eyes going square and your brain turning to mulch. What I worry about more is how plugged into our phones your mother and I must seem to be. You have such little sense of what it is that we are busying ourselves with, and yet multiple times a day you must look up to find me intently searching the object in my hand, tapping at its surface like a mad crow pecking its reflection in a fragment of smashed up wing mirror.

Do you know what the internet is? Like the sky, or language, or the rest of the world that you have not been to, it has always been there. I was twenty-one when I first had my own laptop with an internet connection. Now I long for the quiet situation of being *only in the room*, though I am addicted to waving from my little windows. Is that what the internet is like for you: a vague sense that other people are always there, and that we talk to them, that they carry our attention elsewhere, in a wordless, private haunting?

*

The term 'singularity' might be most commonly associated with black holes, but increasingly you hear it being used as a metaphor relating to technological advancement. The mathematician John von Neumann was the first to assign this definition to singularity: a point at which technology becomes so advanced that it transcends the human intellect. This singularity is therefore synonymous with the arrival of superintelligence, but it also imagines a situation where computers not only outperform all human cognitive capabilities, but are able to develop and engineer new capabilities, resulting in rapidly accelerating self-improvement and subsequent generational development, further and further beyond our understanding.

The most well-known theorist of the technological singularity is Ray Kurzweil, who argues in his 2005 book *The Singularity Is Near* that

> within several decades information-based technologies will encompass all human knowledge and proficiency, ultimately including the pattern-recognition powers, problem-solving skills, and emotional and moral intelligence of the human brain itself.

Kurzweil sets out a compelling and imaginative futurist vision. I don't know enough about nanotech, computing or robotics to be a convert or a sceptic, and the ethical questions arising from his predictions already test the limits of my lowly human hardware. I suppose that is the point: that the technological singularity is an event horizon we are unable to see beyond, but our enhanced descendants, be they machine or human, will inhabit such positions naturally. Perhaps they will struggle to imagine the world as we encounter it now, so slow and in such low resolution.

When I think about what a thought is, maybe 'the language part' of experience (?), I struggle to see how superintelligence can avoid operating at the same representational remove from reality as our own conscious minds: surely superintelligence is not a transcendence of human intelligence altogether, but rather a computerised capacity to represent things more and more quickly? Is greater processing speed actually an increase in the knowledge-making function, or is that a misunderstanding of what knowledge is? In other words, if no human mind is there to interpret the computation, is all that information, abstractly muttering autonomously across the atoms of nanochips, any different from the information stored in a rock? Does knowing more things more quickly make them any more known? Does an increased efficiency in knowing automatically amount to 'progress' or is information something very different from knowledge, which is precisely and only a human paramour? Can we have a more efficient life experience? Efficient in which direction? All directions? Would that be better? We'll have to see. The singularity is predicted to occur very soon. We are speaking on the uncertain threshold.

*

In her famous 1984 essay 'A Cyborg Manifesto', Donna Haraway makes 'an argument for *pleasure* in the confusion of boundaries and for *responsibility* in their construction'. She describes a situation in which

> machines have made thoroughly ambiguous the difference between natural and artificial, mind and body, self-developing and externally designed, and many other distinctions that used to apply to organisms and machines.

'[In] our time, a mythic time,' Haraway continues, 'we are all chimeras, theorized and fabricated hybrids of machine and organism'. It is the figure of the cyborg, 'a creature in a postgender world', who is best positioned to navigate this new terrain. The cyborg is an agent of transcendence and neitherness, whose presence interrupts 'racist, male-dominant capitalism' through its 'partiality, irony, intimacy, and perversity'. It is 'oppositional, utopian, and completely without innocence.'

Cyborgism, in Haraway's terms, offers a positive metaphor for the increasing imperceptibility of our interface with technology; her cyborg is a figure naturally situated within uncertainty, and so able to excite revolutionary and ontological potential. And yet, thirty-seven years have passed since Haraway's manifesto was written – it is as old as I am – Cyborgism is not just a dream of the future, but the story of our past as well. We evolved long ago to be tool users, finding instruments and mechanisms to transcend our physiological limitations and difficulties, from hand-axes, bows and arrows and walking sticks to the light bulb or the pacemaker or even anti-depressants; where does the body

end and technology begin? Were we ever so fixed and imperme-
able to begin with?

The Cyborg Jillian Weise – who uses the pronouns Cy/she/
her – writes about her cyborg identity in her poems and essays.
For her, Haraway's essay

> co-opts cyborg identity while eliminating reference to disabled
> people on which the notion of the cyborg is premised. Disabled
> people who use tech to live are cyborgs. Our lives are not
> metaphors.

It is a vitally important point; people currently reliant on technological aids to stay alive often face a daily battle for visibility,
access and equal rights; if you already possess those rights, and
move around a world designed with your able body in mind,
claiming to be cyborg would be an offensive erasure of the
actual cyborg experience. Those people who use tech to live are
particular knowers; their use of prosthetic technology is a significant subjective factor in the process by which they encounter
the world, and their prosthetics are not just tools for movement,
or for sustaining the body, they are also tools for knowledge-
making.

*

The SynCardia Total Artificial Heart has so far been successfully
transplanted into more than 1,700 patients worldwide awaiting
human donor hearts, including one patient who was supported
by the heart for over four and a half years.

The design of artificial limbs is now so advanced that some
models can be 3D printed for under fifty pounds, and in the
future – using a new technique involving the suturing of graft
'agonist' and 'antagonist' muscles to the end of severed nerve
endings – controlling prosthetics will involve the receiving and

sending of signals to and from the brain; this will mean that users will feel the limbs' positions, their speed and force of movement, in much the same way as if they had an organic limb.

Meanwhile, at De Montfort University, Joan Taylor, a professor of pharmaceutics, is working with a team of researchers on the development of an artificial pancreas, an 'implantable and refillable device that will hold several weeks' insulin supply at a time and make automatic adjustments for the insulin dose needed to control blood glucose levels'.

At Harvard's Wyss Institute for Biologically Inspired Engineering, scientists have now developed a 'biospleen', an external dialysis device that filters out pathogens and toxins from the bloodstream. They have modified a human protein that naturally attaches itself to infectious agents, so that it sticks to the surfaces of magnetic nanobeads that can be introduced into the bloodstream; as infected blood is drawn from the body and passed through their specially developed filter, its magnets simply hoover out the nanobeads, removing with them any infectious agents now glued to their surfaces by the proteins, before the clean blood is returned.

Scientists at the University of Bristol have also been able to manufacture healthy blood from scratch, by halting the life cycle of blood-producing stem cells before these cells decline and die. The new 'immortal' stem cells can therefore continue to produce new blood cells for much longer. The process is very expensive, so its immediate application is more suited to the development of 'designer blood' for specific groups of people or to treat specific conditions, like sickle cell disease; but there is widespread hope that, having discovered the tools for producing new, clean, blood, a cheaper manufacturing process is an achievable next step. Life, for many people, will be known differently.

*

I forget I have a body when I am writing. I disappear from the room and travel here, into my thinking voice. My speaking voice is my body's voice, and I am pretty ambivalent about it. I find the experience of hearing it played back to me unpleasant, if not uncanny. I mean, it's fine. It's home. But I prefer my thinking voice, which I keep indoors, and when I write my thinking voice becomes my voice in a full and total way. I can hear it but also I can't. I'm listening to it right now, but it's more like I am situated in it. Do you know what I mean? I expect you do. I expect that as you read this, your own thinking voice will be intoning on my behalf, tracking the shape, the little melody, of these sentences – not my voice, but a recital in your own. I think that's incredible. I find the idea of that intimacy totally radical and beautiful, but I also find it very funny for reasons I don't quite understand. Hello! It's me! Hahaha.

There is some debate about whether the practice of reading in one's head is something literate humans have always done, or if it is a relatively recent development. In St Augustine's *Confessions*, he notes of Ambrose, Bishop of Milan, that

When he read, his eyes scanned the page and his heart explored the meaning, but his voice was silent and his tongue was still.

That St Augustine saw Ambrose's silent reading as remarkable in the fifth century suggests that it was still unusual at that time. Some scholars refute this, suggesting that sharing what you were reading was the social convention for a time, when literacy was less common; St Augustine comments on the bishop's silence because he sees it as an act of rudeness or secrecy.

Personally I prefer the version where for hundreds of years people bellowed every written word, unaware of the alternative, though I am also loathe to deprive our ancestors of their thinking voices.

*

Six months after you were born I started having panic attacks. They were not frequent, and many of them only gnawed away, refusing to surface beyond a thrum, a foreboding. When an attack did happen it was most commonly at night, after an hour or so of sleep or anxious half-sleep. I would find my body in a state of emergency, my heart pleading, pleading, for me to run away, or do something, anything. My vision felt like it was folding inwards, as if I was permanently on the verge of fainting. I felt that I could not catch my breath, not fully, and the dread that had squatted in me for days ruptured into visions and flashes of thought.

I would tell myself over and over that *this is not a heart attack you are not having a heart attack*, a mantra I soon learned to replace with *you are having a panic attack you are having a panic attack*, though I really didn't want to be having one of those either. I remember that a few times the urge to get up and walk around was so overwhelming I thought I would be sick from resisting it, and so would pace around the room, stopping every few laps to put my hands to my forehead or onto the table, wanting desperately to cry, beckoning that flood, anything other than that agonising, directionless slow detonation, with nowhere to go and nothing to do.

Then one day I decided to pick up my notebook and begin writing. Slowly, I settled, my breathing regulated, my thoughts took shape, giving direction to my feelings; finding my thinking voice was like opening an enormous valve through which the whole weather front inside of me could be steadily decompressed, then released and aimed down the length of my pen, dispersing on the page as soft as rain.

*

Who am I? I have asked that question a lot more since you were born. But the mind turned inwards isn't especially well equipped to make healthy or accurate self-assessments. We only have our hopeful lanterns. Maybe anxiety makes us alert to the tenuousness of our self-performance. Brittle, fraudulent, every sentence or small gesture can seem histrionic under the heat lamp of such uncharitable scrutiny.

> We are made up of the same atoms and the same light signals
> as are exchanged between pine trees in the mountains and stars
> in the galaxies,

writes Carlo Rovelli. Photons and neutrinos whoosh through us, even in the womb; my thinking voice is the result of energy being exchanged on a molecular level. And then it is estimated that the average human body contains at least as many foreign cells as those deriving from our own DNA. The highest estimate puts the ratio at just one human cell for every ten cells of human microbiota: foreign bacteria, viruses, fungi, archaea and protists. It's a well-known fact that the adult human body is 60% water, but it also seems to be made up of a kind of clever imported yoghurt. And although the popular myth that 'we replace every cell in our body every seven years' is untrue, our body is nevertheless in constant flux, some of our cells *are* being replaced all the time. Some of our brain cells have been alive for as long as we have. Others will be born so close to our time of death that they will outlive us by minutes, hours, maybe even a day or two: lonely witnesses to the end of their world.

*

In the film *Amour* (2012), a terminally ill woman is looking through an album of old photographs. She remarks that life is 'so beautiful'

– and so long.

84

When you were born, we made a group photo album that we could upload pictures to, for sharing with grandparents and family. I wander into it often. There are so many pictures and videos.

here you are the first time I held you;
here you are in the hospital cot the night we didn't sleep;
here you are in the car seat on the way home;
here you are meeting the cat;
here you are two months old strapped into a harness on my
    chest as I
trudge through snow to the shops, your first snow, snow
    you have no
memory of;
here you are, a godlet of porridge, your spoon aloft, your
    face entirely
covered;
here you are looking cross on the anti-Trump march;
here you are saying *church, steeple, doors, people* . . . along
    with the rhyme while
I sign it out for you;
here you are in the arms of your mother your faces both
    lit up by the
firework display;
here, in a tent;
here, your hair in plaits for the first time;
on the beach just last week . . .

Life, so beautiful – so long!

A thousand days
how slowly

how always
and often
I've lost you
to the losing.

*

Technology is complicating our experience as knowers, and that complication extends to how we know ourselves. Social media profiles help us construct and present the appearance that we are continuous subjects moving through the world, but such constructions are a constant reminder that we are unfinished. They produce in us this a churning need to be verified. Like the electrons that power our phones, it is as if we only materialise into existence when coming into contact with someone else. Our intersubjectivity is so tangible now, and it takes place synonymously and in parallel with ad campaigns, the content and copy we curate *about* ourselves.

Reading ourselves and each other is tiring work and I do not think we are even close to understanding what this new demand is doing to us. I feel fatigued by the obligation to present myself fit for broadcast, and I worry what it is doing to us as knowers. We human beings have always located ourselves through a process of relation, in poses, gestures, signals, and codes. But what about the respite of solitude? One can take a little holiday, delete the apps, drown the router in the bathtub, but how has disconnecting become a conscious choice we have to take rather than the other way around? The work of self-knowledge, and knowing others, isn't getting easier, even if technology is providing us with the tools to do it more immediately and with more and more people simultaneously. We have the potential for much wider connectivity, our thoughts and voices reaching further than we are able to predict or control, but this potential comes with the attendant anxiety of exposure, a sense of vulnerability or pre-emptive defensiveness. I have learned an enormous amount through social media. It has given me access to a broader range of voices and experiences, challenging my empathetic imagination, my ignorance and my lazy assumptions about people. But I worry that the scale of interaction requires more of us emotionally than we are aware, and that while we police and attend to our growing public lives with greater fluency, we have less energy to spend on privately reckoning with our failures and fears, and learning to inhabit the versions of ourselves to which we aspire.

*

The surgeon Sergio Canavero believes that he is now able to transplant the head of a living patient onto the dead body of a donor. By using a fusogen compound called polyethylene glycol, Canavero believes he can reattach the brain by fusing it to the donor's spinal cord. Canavero works closely with Xiaoping Ren, an orthopaedic surgeon from China's Harbin Medical University, who has already performed head-transplant operations on more than a thousand mice, though these have not survived for longer than a few minutes. Ren and Canavero have also attempted head-transplant procedures on a dog, a monkey and a human cadaver – or I should say on dogs, monkeys and human cadavers (plural), rather than a monstrous combination of all three. They even had a willing trial subject, Valery Spiridonov, who was prepared to undergo the pioneering procedure, but after falling in love, marrying, and becoming a father for the first time he decided to withdraw from the trial programme in 2019.

While Canavero himself remains optimistic about finding a new candidate and proceeding with his research, he has also admitted that a person with a transplanted head (or should it be transplanted body?) would only be 10–15% neurofunctional, which, combined with a very high risk of death during or soon after the procedure, raises ethical questions about its supposed viability or potential 'success'. The spinal cord is responsible for transmitting vital information to the brain, giving us sensation, as well as proprioception, which tells us where we are in relation to our surroundings. Given that there is no guarantee of such capabilities being returned, can the transplant be classified as a medical undertaking with the patient's needs in mind, or isn't it more of an experiment to test surgical capability?

Beyond questions of procedural viability lie numerous philosophical, ethical, economic and medical questions about head transplantation which also need to be considered. Firstly, is our head really so autonomous an object that *we* would actually survive its transplantation? Our brains have developed in conversation with our very specific physiology. In fact, the mind and the body are not separate at all, but part of a complementary system in constant discourse, feeding back and sending out, interpreting, responding and manufacturing each other in concert. Adaptable as the organ of the brain is, could it really survive such a brutal segue in its experience, without significant changes in personality, cognition, apprehension? This is before you factor in the significant psychological impact of such a surgery and the uncanny reality of its aftermath: being conjoined to a body that has already lived a life of it's own.

The body comprises, on average, upwards of 80% of a person's mass. Does most of what makes us a person really live in the 20% above the neck? What is to say that, rather than saving the person in the head, a transplant would not actually result in the creation of a third person: a new knower? What if the new knower rejects the old knowledge in the head, refuses their name, their family, wants to start again? Should society grant them that freedom and allow them to simply wander into a future cleaved of its anterior? Where might we then say that the old person, or old people, went? Do we mourn them? Has the knower who entered

squeezed, the water absorbed by the large intestine and the thick, turdy waste jollied on towards your rectum, itself a manifold system of muscles and nerves that you have trained now to halt and release. You were quick to get the hang of it, those muscles. You are so clever on the potty. How proud I am of your big-girl pants. Really quite astounding.

I remember when you had two teeth. It was hilarious to brush them, your front guys. Now you have the full set and we take turns – you for ten seconds, me for ten seconds – for as long as you can bear to sit still. I remember when you started on solids, how swallowing made you gag and choke, how we watched a YouTube tutorial to learn the baby version of the Heimlich manoeuvre: face down along the thighs with the head hanging over the knees, a firm pat pat pat. I imagined myself doing it, imagined you choking, over and over, like a tongue perversely returning to the ulcer in the footwell between gum and lip. I must have cut a thousand grapes in half since then.

I know your body better than my own. Every day I watch over it, lift it, swing it high into the air, or pin it, tickling squeals and chuckles out of the head end of it. I've held you, feverish and sweaty, waiting for the Calpol to kick in. I've placed my mobile phone to your lips so a man could count your breaths, then carried it into the taxi to hospital, because it was New Year's Eve and all the ambulances were taken. I've watched your body sleep, beneath the gaze of a huge purple octopus painted on the wall of the children's A & E, while other, sicker, kids sat crying, shivering, coughing, your fever already broken, 6 a.m., several milligrams of ibuprofen later and 2019 was underway, a bleary yellow sun leaking through the mist on Woolwich common. Relief, my favourite emotion.

Once, playing in a garden somewhere, you fell and cut your lip. I picked you up and held your head to my shoulder. I could feel your blood blotting my T-shirt before I saw it. Not much, but I knew my T-shirt was getting ruined. I did not care. So utterly did not care, I think I even wanted my T-shirt to be ruined.

*

Is my thinking voice a technology from outside or inside my body? When I'm writing a poem, my thinking voice becomes the voice of the poem. My thinking voice is organised into a body of its own, designed to be more permanent. My thinking voice becomes the voice of the poem which is a robot experiencing the sensation of being me, a replica with its own timeline, divergent, pliable and built to outlive me, to inhabit other multiple bodies.

*

Hello. It's your thinking voice
speaking I've been thinking
of a flower garland given
as a gift to the intersubjective
if you follow it's already
in your hand pink and red
and coral with the scent
of your tongue's interior.

Conjoin with me a while.
Now, when I
say *I*
I
mean you
to follow
me when I
say *you*
I mean you
to follow me.

Do you follow me?
Like a bird in your attic?

You can only live for ever
by staying in the present
by which point your body
has moved on.
Go then.
Move your body on.
Don't worry about me.
I'm uploaded here.

VI.

THE NEW LIFE

For people like us who believe in physics, the separation between past, present and future has only the importance of an admittedly tenacious illusion.

– Albert Einstein

You are going through a phase where, if you do something naughty or become overwhelmed or upset, you ask that we go back and start over. You refuse the linearity of time, and demand the right to edit and reroute the past in order to free your present of causality and consequence.

The other day you went mad because you couldn't put your own socks on correctly. I tried to calm you down and asked you what the matter was, but nothing could amend the error, the future was broken, the only way forwards was backwards. I asked if you wanted to *start again from the beginning*, and immediately it calmed you. I took the socks and went back upstairs. Then, after observing a ten-second silence on the landing, I came back down, announcing cheerily that I had your socks and we could put them on together. Your eyes were still a little red from crying, but you were delighted, and calmly we started over.

I do not know if indulging this demand is healthy, or whether it is founded in denial and I am actually encouraging you to be less conscientious. It has an element of play about it – we both know that the rerun is less authentic, although we don't acknowledge it directly. I can see a negative side to pretending that *what has happened has not happened* but if it enables you to learn more easily through failure, through experimentation, then I don't really mind.

*

Most poets, I think, keep multiple drafts of the poem they are writing – 'Final version 7' and 'Final version 7 FINAL' – as a safeguard against the casual brutality of editing: you can nudge things around for an hour, and without really meaning to you have murdered not just your darlings, as they say, but their pets and relatives too.

With multiple drafts you can pretend that timeline didn't happen. You can simply go back upstairs, count to ten and re-emerge with the same socks as before. I don't do that. I keep one draft, and if I ruin it ... well, never mind. I like knowing that decisions have consequences. I do what I think is right at the time, and trust myself. You can usually salvage a few scraps for repurposing, so what's the big deal? Maybe I need the fear, the slight risk, to force myself to take responsibility for the poem in my care. If I can't fuck it up then nothing matters, so I have to move forwards, from decision to decision, in one vulnerable, resolute trajectory.

*

In the famous paradox of Zeno of Elea (c. 490 to c. 430 BC), a flying arrow is found to be *always at rest*, because at any point during its flight it can be said to occupy a certain point in time and space. In order for an arrow to be *somewhere* at a given instant, it needs must be stationary. It must occupy that space at that time and only that space, so how can the arrow also be in motion if it continually occupies these fixed positions? The paradox draws attention to the fact that time cannot be stopped at x to fix the arrow in its position y.

An arrow flies a finite distance over a finite timescale, because the scale of measurement we impose upon it is finite. In reality there is no finite system of measurement, and so there cannot be fixed instants in time and space. To have a *point* in time, like a coordinate, would mean that no time is elapsing, which is no time at all. At best, an instant can be theorised as an infinitesimally small interval or chunk, which can theoretically be *taken out* of the continuous flow of time, and then divided infinitely, collapsing inwards as we refine and refine our units of measurement, making them smaller and smaller. But these infinitesimal slices are still not points, still not zero: they are intervals within which the arrow can travel; the only limit is the scale of our measurement.

*

The game involved my brother or me climbing on top of something not too high, like a sofa, or a tree stump, and asking Dad to catch us. He would get into position and say, 'Go on! Jump! I'll catch you,' and every time we leapt, he'd back away and let us fall. Because he let us fall each time we kept trying, demanding new assurances, squinting and giggling as we scrutinised his face. He'd be already laughing as he said it again, 'Go on! Jump! I'll catch you.' He never caught us, and never would catch us, and that, we soon understood, was the whole point of the game, and why we insisted on playing it.

*

I remind my dad about the game, and he feels guilty:

I must have caught you once or twice?!

But I don't remember being caught. I only remember wanting to try again, to test the law, as if I were climbing to a mountaintop to demand that God speak to me, so that I might confirm my disbelief by the silence that followed, a silence bigger than God, an absence more miraculous.

I wanted to be caught, but being caught would end the game, would break its only rule, which was the whole game: an inverted trust exercise, a test of my unconditionality, my determination and resilience, but also a little disappointing to discover I would fall and fall for ever.

A child is falling.
When did the falling begin?

All my life a moment ago
I occupied a certain space
of inward long division.
Does the horizon rise
that I might step beyond it?
My arms outstretched, a beat,
a breath and jumping not
to be caught but to fall,
a child continuously at rest
catching myself again today
taking to the earth.

*

The fog recedes to reveal a coastline: the permanence of our new situation: the rest of your life and the rest of ours.

It was hard to come to terms with, and we even talked about *the old life* longingly, openly, unashamedly. How beautiful and hungover our eternal Sundays. How deliciously self-centred we could permit ourselves to be. I don't mean that having a child has made us more caring or generous people – God, I don't believe that at all – just that, before, we only had each other's needs to consider; needs we could barter for and align according to each of our preferences. Now everything is triangulated via your needs, and you have needed us so completely and relentlessly. If anything parenthood has made us more selfish, more insular, always directing our heart's resources inwards, our love a burning boat. Speaking as a parent, there is nothing about parenthood that extends the reach and breadth of your capability to love beyond the inner machinery of the family, or endows you with special insight into the lives of others. It does not make you wiser about anything apart from the experience that you have had. That is still wisdom earned, still experience and learning and knowledge gained, but the intensity and value of all of it springs from its particularity. What fresh understanding you have is only applicable within the confines of the family paddock. In that sense parenthood makes being a good person in a broader sense much harder, and it certainly gives you less time and energy for the enterprise.

*

Henri Bergson, born in Paris in 1859, enlivened Cartesian philosophy, which assumes that the mind is separate from the world, by arguing that the concept of time, as a physical quantity divisible into measurable units, is an illusion entirely constructed and upheld by the intellect. He posited duration as a fluid, fugitive concept, where the past is manifested in the present, which is not a 'now' moment endlessly disappearing, but a threshold of constant becoming. While the striking of a clock can demarcate a supposedly fixed point in time, duration cannot be analysed or understood in terms of static 'points' or 'instants', but is the continuum of time as we experience or intuit it, with the help of clocks or without them.

Bergson was a famous and enigmatic intellectual figure, drawing enormous, traffic-jamming crowds to his lectures. His thinking around time was perceived as controversial, not least because it directly challenged Einstein's revolutionary new general theory of relativity. In the early twentieth century, the prevalence of accurate clocks, the introduction of time zones and the organisation of mass industrial infrastructure meant that time needed to be regulated, simultaneous. Bergson's theory of duration provocatively suggested that a regularised idea of time gives an insufficient account of time's nature and our relationship to it. What Bergson was seeking was something like a reconciliation between the material, positivist conception of time as objectively measurable, and the psychological or durational experience of time and its intuition. He argued that time, understood as a physical quantity, is a reduction useful for social organisation, but that time's true nature includes us, springs from us, and so he defined time as uncertain, as belonging to that confusion.

For Einstein, this was unacceptable. He admitted privately that Bergson understood his general theory of relativity, and was therefore qualified to critique it, but publicly demanded that the human intellect be kept separate from its scientific description, which could be tested and proven by the measurement of clocks, and theorised in mathematical equations. Einstein believed that time can take place regardless of our existence, and be used to extend our understanding of the mathematical universe, whereas for Bergson time is not Platonic; it cannot be cleaved from perception or subjectivity. Time is an extension of us, a product of our thinking and feeling.

Bergson was not hostile to the mathematics of the general theory of relativity. He was a mathematician himself, and observed that

No physics, no astronomy, no science is possible if we deny the scientist the right to represent the whole universe schematically on a piece of paper.

But he would not accept the reductivism of the theory that time belongs to clocks, as if they could describe time by themselves, and are not, instead, tools precisely designed to designate perceivable events and moments of simultaneity.

Bergson's thinking threatened to undermine Einstein's whole project, because if time does correspond to subjectivity, if a *knowing of time* depends in any way on *the knower*, then nothing objective or universal can be known about time at all. If, as Bergson claimed, Einstein's theory 'pertains essentially to epistemology', then time is not merely a matter for physics, but also a valid subject of debate by philosophers. This might seem like a minor detail, but it introduced a significant element of doubt around Einstein's theoretical masterpiece. When Einstein was awarded the Nobel Prize in Physics it was for 'his services to theoretical physics, and especially for his discovery of the law of the photoelectric effect', and not for his general theory of relativity; and while the Nobel panel must have had various reasons – given the rigours and complexities of its deliberations – the prize committee chairman himself noted in his award speech that 'it will be no secret that the famous philosopher Bergson in Paris has challenged this theory'. Bergson had not disproved Einstein's theory of relativity, but he does appear to have kept the importance of human experience in play when it came to the description of time's nature.

*

Poems are durational. How could they be otherwise? Even when they march forwards according to a regular metre, they are so full of echo, so frequently bringing the past into the present. Take metaphor – 'the sun is a blood orange': each word happens in a fixed order, and yet the sentence calls back to itself, its resolution reimagining its beginning. It moves forwards into the past. Or think about poetic musicality, how rhythm bids us search for the shape of the past in each new phrase, and so each line arrives already haunted, and haunts in turn the lines that will follow. Or how rhyme completes its intervals within and across the sentences that hold it; how even sentences, their syntax and lean, can lag and bend into the present: you can load up a sentence on one side like this, and already you know that after the pivot, here, the sentence will now head downhill, towards its destination, with a slightly falling intonation, and a pleasurable sense of equilibrium when it locates its end, as if you had just carried a tray of drinks across a room, anticipating the moment you will set it down. We have heard the song of so many different kinds of sentence that we know, more or less, how they will play out, at least in terms of their musical shape. Sentences also have the interruptions of the poetic line to contend with. The double halt of an end stop, or the cliff edge of a line break midway. A line break makes for a further visual grammar of delay and revelation, take-offs and landings, meting out each episode of drama, image and sound.

Then there's the fact that poems are commonly held to be rereadable objects, so the whole longer sequence of the poem is played over, layered, taken out of order, the sustain pedal held down; the individual notes become the one great chord of the thing, reverberating.

In fact, a poem can feel so durational that it seems to take place outside of time altogether, a kind of forever-present. Like an epistle or soliloquy delivered from within some infinitesimally small interval, beyond perception or measurement. At the same time, a poem can feel as if it was always there, glaciers gushing and foaming around it, geology blooming and laying its blankets down, waiting to be discovered by the poet, like a piece of maths for the realist mathematician. I don't know, it's fanciful. But the experience of reading or writing a poem can be like an extraction from life, or a re-situation into it.

Poetic experiences can be like that too. A kind of cinematic whooshing-out, a self-consciousness about *being*, in relation not just to the rest of your own life gone and before you, but the lives of others too, and beyond, into history and prehistory, the ancient night sky so oblivious to everything you will ever think or feel that to even suggest its awareness exposes the inescapable sentimentalism of your perspective and laughable inadequacy of your vision and ability to imagine beyond the confines of your lived reality. I can feel like that looking at a pot plant. Thousands of years of evolution and reproduction, cells knocking and bumping and dying, and here we are, two organisms burning up our precious seconds of existence, our bodies attending passionately to themselves, the sun swinging by each day, and yet, for all this talk and fear and love and grief, we are so far, far away from approaching the possibility of denting the surface of time as it yawns through the universe. The stakes are so low, they couldn't be higher. I sigh at the thought, the little reconnection between the summative fragments of song that my whole life will gather, and the whole rest of everything. We're nearly nothing at all, so small, and yet not zero. Still time enough for an arrow to keep moving. 'How – I didn't know any / word for it – how "unlikely" ...' as Elizabeth Bishop writes in her poem 'In the Waiting Room':

> I was saying it to stop
> the sensation of falling off
> the round, turning world,
> into cold, blue-black space.

I think that's a perfect description of writing a poem too: demarcating the specifics of this great, wide unlikelihood, to stop for a moment, to stop the sensation that you are falling off the world.

*

We tend to think of language as accrued, word by word, gathering and mutating over millennia. But words are not the full story of language, not at all. Words are only one strain of the vast human refinement and diversification of a far earlier impulse: meaning to mean. When did articulacy and intention begin?

What was that first act of conscious representation? A mating call in the Palaeozoic era? A prehistoric cry for help? A dinosaur making a sound of gratitude or pleasure? We know that it must have started at some point, because the concept of a 'point' in time is evidence of the system itself. Like a black hole accruing mass around itself, that point in time when language started must also be a singularity of sorts.

Maybe this applies to knowledge too: at a 'certain point' a creature or person felt in some way that they knew something, and from there knowledge began to happen. Not as a moth's journey towards a singular, bright truth, but as a wild refinement and diversification of knowledges in all directions. I suspect not. Not if a 'certain point in time' does not exist beyond the remit of the human intellect and its practical, reasonable divisions. Maybe that was the first piece of knowledge, a *here* to occupy, a feeling of presence, of time passing, and from that feeling knowledge could begin.

*

[*Shh!* A poem is taking place]

> For six whole days the storm refused us,
> air gone creepy and aroused

                              an unbreaking fever
                          on the warm window panes . . .

[Time kept general]

                          Now heavy rain darkens the driveway
                            and the trees that line the driveway
                               and the gaps between the trees
                              that line the driveway to the road
                               the road lying down a dying man
                     in the wind an oral history of the river

[Then suddenly]

                                   Fourteen years have passed
                                    and we don't look the same.
                                                        You say
                           That storm was before I was born, dad,
                                     why do you keep on warning me?
                                 Because it wasn't that kind of storm.
                               And this isn't that kind of warning.

                                          *

Despite all the love we had ready for you in the new life, we
worried so much that we would fuck you up. It was as if you
arrived with your whole future in tow. I remember taking
you home from the hospital and feeling that there should have
been more paperwork. We signed a form or two and then they
just sort of let us take you away. A human child. Then, when we
got home and parenthood got underway, it was as if a container
vessel had been moored up overnight on the street outside,
filled with thirty thousand tons of documentation pertaining
to every gesture, act and breath of your life, which was now our
responsibility.

Ah, but you were a delightful baby. Quiet and quizzical and daft and so so determined. And the joy was intoxicating; exactly like being in love, that bottomless yearning for what we already had. There were also the periods when for nights on end you would wake, and wake, and wake, or wake only once but stay awake for hours, blinking and innocent, or manic and untameable, clambering over our bed, refusing to lie down. In the mornings, partitioned from the drama of the night by only an hour or two of dreamless capitulation-sleep, we would look in the mirror and find two broken, defeated people. It was literally painful to be awake.

You were so tired. You were undergoing a rapid period of neurological maturation, and it left you ragged and emotional, or destructive, bitey and aggressive by day, and at night it was anyone's guess. Your developmental leaps and changes turned your sleep into a puzzle. We would have a week-long run of good nights, and then for no discernible reason or change to our routine you would not or could not settle. And why would you? Your brain was building whole new tenements and avenues. Sometimes you woke in a frenzy, other times you seemed altered, with a creepy, gothic, haunted absence about you, as if you were about to blurt a dark premonition or speak with a voice not your own. I am a relatively rational person, but more than once I considered the possibility of demonic possession. One night, when you were perhaps ten months old, you simply refused to go to sleep. It was 11 p.m. and you were still going, happily playing on the bed. Then, all of a sudden, you stood up. For the first time unaided. You just rose to your feet and stood there. We all froze. You stood there for a full ten seconds, and then we all laughed and cheered. Five minutes later you were asleep.

Our immune systems took a hammering. I remember having a horrible sore throat that persisted for nine weeks. I ate ice lollies for breakfast so that I could talk without wincing. Because there were always symptoms of being run down to contend with, it was easy to quietly convince myself that my physical condition was perilous, that I was dying, and if your mother complained of a headache, a backache, a soreness in her stomach, I searched the dark for diagnoses and gnawed on them too, like a terrible secrets, scaring myself half to tears while solemnly doing the dishes. It was bleak. I was going mad, and I could feel it happening. And yes, I thought about whether I would be happier had you not been born. I think every parent crawls to the edge of that hole, and peers blankly into it. Dim, pointless interrogations that yield only shame and remorse. Of course I didn't want you gone; that was precisely why I was so utterly fucked with worry – I couldn't keep you safe enough. I desperately needed a little ventilation, just to weigh the size of the change. Because everything had changed. A new sky installed. *The New Life*.

Then sleep returned once more to the land. I began to trust you more to survive without my interventions, your autonomy like a fierce chemical reaction, bubbling and foaming, overflowing into the whole flat. What could I do but stand back and watch you forge a temporality of your own, bruising the air with your voice, taking your first steps, upturning furniture, brandishing your future like a red plastic spoon?

And so I started to write again.

*

The representation of time in a text is not regular. Time requires narration. Sometimes texts narrate at odds with time, and at other times texts seem to run simultaneously with time's passing. All first-person texts, for example, are voiced, and so their narration occurs at a rate roughly equivalent to that of the voice speaking or thinking. We could say that the speed of narration is equivalent to the speed of thought, or of voice, events taking place in a kind of rolling present, e.g. 'I am lying here in this hammock wasting my life deliberately.'

Other kinds of texts narrate the passing of time at a much greater rate than it takes to speak or read the narration itself, e.g. 'Fourteen years pass, and the village forgets about the child.'

The sentence only takes a second or two to read, and yet it presents fourteen years' worth of time passing: the text dilates time – fourteen years in three words – whoosh!

But narration is never truly 'unvoiced'; even though we might follow convention and allow the narrator to disappear from our view. But in stories and poems time cannot pass without some form of narration, without language generating its intervals. It requires enormous writerly skill and energy to narrate events seemingly invisibly, inaudibly, as if there were no one there, no one meaning to mean; as if language, which, over a lifetime, we enter into then finally leave, might somehow transcend the page and speak for itself 'unvoiced'. I can only think of one such transcendental narrator, and that narrator is time.

*

Imagine you are all grown-up. Out on your own in the world. You take a train, you have the carriage to yourself, a window seat. On the neighbouring track there is another train. Suddenly it starts to move away, or wait, isn't it your train that's moving? Perhaps, in fact, both trains are moving away from one another, but which is moving faster? In the end, what does it matter? Nothing is stationary, you know that. The universe, the galaxy, the solar system and the earth are all in motion, just as much as your train is. Your train is only moving somewhere relative to somewhere else, and at a time relative to some other time. You can only observe the effects and details of the universe and the appearance of certain phenomena from within your particular reference frame. Everything is relative. Or nearly everything.

The only constant across all reference frames is the speed of light. The speed of light is the thing to hang on to. You can trust it anywhere. But wait: speed involves distance, and time; light must travel in its constant way through something, and that something is spacetime: three-dimensional space plus the fourth dimension, time, all taken together.

What about the light travelling on your train? The light moving through the spacetime of your reference frame? Now that your train is moving, is the light on board the train travelling faster than it was back when you were sitting in the station? Could you toss a ball of light up into the air like an apple now, and catch it in your hand, or would it shoot off faster than light itself? No. The speed of light is constant. It will do what it always does. It will travel at the speed of light, unaffected by the particular reference frame that your moving train represents. The speed of light will demand that the dimensions of time and space change to accommodate its constancy; spacetime will uphold the speed of light through a kind of curvature or distortion: time on board your train will slow down.

Not in a way that you will notice. That much is clear. Your watch will chart its own progress, the window vibrate against your forehead as you lean against it; time will feel normal. And light will appear normal too, constant as always, touching things, the surface of the apple that has rolled out of the top of your bag on the table. Light will behave itself just as it must.

But, if I could see you, somehow, from within my reference frame, sitting here at my desk, while you speed away from me on your high-velocity train, taking your apple in hand to throw yourself a catch, I would see that apple rise and rise into the air, revolving slowly like a moon. I would see the string of spit breaking between your teeth as your mouth opens into a smile, while you wait the long less-than-a-second that it takes for the apple to revolve a couple more times, then begin its descent back to your hand. The speed of light is constant everywhere, but spacetime operates within reference frames relative to velocity. The faster you travel on your train, the more slowly time on your train would appear to pass were I able to observe you from my desk at rest. Einstein called this 'time dilation'.

*

The word 'present' comes from the Latin *prae-*, meaning 'before', and *esse*, meaning 'to be'. To occupy the present is to occupy the *before the to be*. A little trick, to be *here* before the *now*. Hardly here at all. A present presented, but not yet received, because if you have received the present you've already accepted it, carried into the past. Perhaps the present is unrepresentable. To present the unrepresentable is sublime, to paraphrase Jean-François Lyotard. Always before, and always to be: but we can be present, by our presence. Perhaps that is the sublime: presence as a way of representing the unrepresentable, time not passing us by but situated within us.

A Planck time unit is the time it takes for light in a vacuum to travel across a Planck length, which is 1.6 metres divided by ten, 35 times. We cannot conceptualise a measurable increment of time any smaller, so perhaps that is the present.

But we can theorise 'half a Planck', because a Planck length is a number, not a thing. There is a theoretical 'infinity' of distances between 0 and 1 Planck length in numerical terms, and these are not bound by what we can measure. The singularity of a black hole, for example, is infinitely small in theory, and so infinitely smaller than a Planck length, though I don't know if light in a vacuum could ever cross one. The present remains infinitely

111

divisible in theory, but not in a way which is measurable in the real world.

Neuroscientists suggest that the human brain processes a cognitive 'present' in increments of 200 milliseconds, which is a much longer present than Planck's, but still very short. This must mean that any measurable interval of the present shorter than the cognitive present is always already a feature of the past by the time we apprehend it: literally gone before you know it. Not *before the to be*, but after it.

*

Your feet are experiencing a slower version of time than your head, because they are closer to the earth's gravitational centre, according to the report 'Optical Clocks and Relativity' by C. W. Chou et al., who tested the phenomenon. This tallies with what Einstein's theory of time dilation suggests. Time is far from being the regular, standardised thing that we refer to so certainly on a daily basis. The rotation of the earth is slowing. Every few years the International Earth Rotation and Reference Systems Service adds a 'leap second' to Coordinated Universal Time, so that the earth's slowing rotation can 'catch up' with the atomic devices that set the rate at which time is said to pass. Our atomic clocks are too accurate in their regularity for the poor old earth spinning in space. The next date on which a leap second will be added is 30 June 2021, when time will be 'stopped', or rather, when a sixtieth second will be permitted across the globe before the sequential midnight point of each time zone, the time then reading 23:59:60. If you do not add that second to your watch, it will forever be running slow.

*

Maybe time is another singularity, a phenomenon that we know exists because we witness it and are moved by it. Events seem to occur within it, but we will always fall short of a perfect theory

112

because of our own cognitive limitations, which cannot be extracted from time, but rely on it entirely. The philosopher John D. Caputo writes that

if we wait for absolutes to fall from the sky, nothing will ever happen. [. . .] The idea is not to find a midway point between absolutism and relativism but to scuttle entirely that oppositional schema, which has done so much damage. Modernity's obsession with certainty is hard-headed and it's blackmail.

Lorraine Code goes further:

For a relativist, who contends that there can be many valid ways of knowing any phenomenon, there is the possibility of taking several constructions, many perspectives into account. Hence relativism keeps open a range of interpretive possibilities. At the same time, because of the epistemic choices it affirms, it creates stringent accountability requirements of which knowers have to be cognizant. Thus it introduces a moral-political component into the heart of epistemological enquiry.

*

The Big Bang, the very beginning of time, sent everything hurtling outwards. Just as the Doppler effect causes us to hear the siren of an ambulance lowering in pitch as it speeds away from us, scientists have observed a 'redshift' – a lowering in the frequency of electromagnetic wavelengths – in the light sent by objects travelling away from us in outer space; we know that the universe is still expanding.

In the 1990s, it was the generally held view among cosmologists that the universe did not contain enough mass to 'crunch' back inwards again; instead, the universe would continue expanding forever, though the gravity of its mass would slow the rate of that outward expansion. Yet now there is enormous uncertainty and disagreement about the rate of the universe's expansion, because astronomers are finding that it is in fact accelerating. In 1998, a survey of distant supernovae by an international team of astronomers found that the light emitted by these huge exploding stars was fainter than it should be, or rather, reaching Earth from further away than it should. The survey was met with scepticism, but soon other astronomers returned similar results. By the turn of the millennium, astronomers had not only found that the universe is accelerating outwards, but that this follows an initial period of deceleration lasting until seven billion years after the Big Bang. The reason for this behaviour remains unknown.

One theory is the existence of dark energy, a repulsive force counteracting the attractive force of gravity, similar to that which Einstein offered as an explanation for the universe's expansion at a time when he still contested the validity of the Big Bang model. Since then, the Big Bang has become the dominant theory of how the universe was created, and now dark energy, once proposed by Einstein as something of a theoretical fudge, is thought to comprise as much as 68% of matter in the universe.

But recently, the dark energy theory has been contested by the physicists José Senovilla, Marc Mars and Raül Vera, who suggest that, rather than the universe expanding at faster and faster rates, what we are actually seeing is time itself slowing down; the impression of acceleration is an illusion. They believe that those who have calculated that the expansion of the universe is accelerating have done so based on the assumption that time is constant throughout the universe, when, at its outer most reaches, time is actually degrading.

If time is slowing down, does it mean it could stop altogether? This seems preposterous, until one remembers that it is generally accepted that the Big Bang brought about the beginning of time, so this radical theory is in many ways the same idea playing out in reverse.

Meanwhile, the physicists Davide Fiscaletti, Amrit Sorli and Dusan Klinar have posited that time has no primary physical existence at all. In order to measure motion and frequency we can generate a t axis on a graph to plot and chart the variables, but these pertain only to a mathematical value. It is as if we overlaid time onto motion, as something separate to motion, in order to describe how things move mathematically, but time is not a physical entity or part of the real system in play. In this sense, the universe is timeless. We can stop thinking of time as anything other than the numbers we assign to motion. This means no arrow paradox, no time dilation, no dimension but that which manifests in the physical world.

*

There is a comb in the bathroom, carved from a cow horn into the shape of a horse. Yesterday you asked me where it came from. When I told you that your mother and I bought it on holiday when we were much younger, you looked puzzled.

Was I there?
No, this was before you were born.
Where was I?
You didn't exist yet.
Did I go on the plane?
No, you were . . .

I couldn't find a way of explaining the time before you, and part of me felt cruel even suggesting it existed, as if that state of not yet being was a kind of death before life. I could tell that you already felt left out of the experience, or perhaps you feared that we had abandoned you without your knowing.

It can't be coincidence that recently you have started remembering events with more clarity. It is as if the infant memory, spongey and fluent in patterns and repetition, has subsided, and what has replaced it is a firmer, more wrought and self-conscious kind of memory. Your mind before made everything a game, as if primarily geared towards learning sequences. Now you want singular occurrences, anecdotes, causality and specificity. Your personhood feels more ornate, defined and solid too, and you seem to be drawing from intervals of weeks, rather than days, for frames of reference. When you were an infant your future was right in front of your face, then, when you became a toddler, it stretched into the afternoon. Now that you are nearly three you ask what we will do tomorrow. You want plans, you remind me of the last time we went into town, the ice cream you ate on the bench with me, while I held one hand over your head to protect you from the falling acorns, and mopped at your fingers and mouth with a wipe in my other. It is as if you have woken up more, your mind is expanding, and the rate of that expansion is accelerating. At the same time, your infantile past is more vague, misty, unreliable. I ask if you remember last Christmas, and I can tell that you are as much inventing it as you are remembering. *Do you remember the tree?* I ask, and you smile. Yes, you remember the tree. You spend a second or two letting the memory illuminate your brain, and I can see from your expression that the recollection is growing more vivid. Then, suddenly, you look to me for reassurance. Yes, I smile back, a tree indoors, covered in lights, that really happened.

*

It has long been recognised that our experience of time involves temporal distortions caused by our emotional state, along with numerous other factors, such as illness, tiredness and the familiarity of the activity we are undertaking. Neurologists and psychologists have proven in numerous studies that an excitement in our emotional state causes us to overestimate the amount of time elapsing. Time seems to pass more slowly in a car travelling towards the edge of a cliff than it does in a car being driven away from it, for example.

We also tend to overestimate the duration of our exposure to unfamiliar items, especially when they are introduced into a set pattern of familiar ones; repetition comparably compresses our experience of time, whereas the appearance of an 'oddball' in a sequence has the effect of slowing time down. Interestingly, a 2015 study by Mingbo Cai, David M. Eagleman and Wei Ji Ma found that 'perceived duration is reduced by repetition but not by high-level expectation', meaning that less frequent repetition in a standard sequence actually has a more pronounced effect on the perceived compression of time. In other words, being able to predict a repetition counteracts the compression of time that repetition otherwise causes.

In a further twist, a 2018 study by Mohammad Ali Nazari et al. showed that the slowing of psychological time does not happen as much for trained musicians. They report that, while for non-musicians

a higher degree of oddball deviancy results in a greater dilation of perceived duration [. . .] there is neither a position nor a deviancy effect with musician participants; the subjective duration remains constant.

Musicians experience a more regular sense of time than non-musicians. This is a bit of mess, isn't it? No wonder we rely on mechanically regulated time so much to regularise our lives. But what causes this variability, not just between one person and another, but within individuals, between one activity and another? One theory is that the appearance of an oddball item triggers an increase in the rate at which we process information in the brain – a little burst of urgency – and it is this increased rate that expands our subjective sense of time passing.

Another theory, developed in the 1970s by John Gibbon, then professor of psychology at Columbia University, is that the brain possesses an internal clock, a discrete pacemaker, which emits pulses, and that we accumulate these pulses as we apprehend something. Originally devised to describe animal behaviour, Gibbon's Scalar Expectancy Theory has since been used to explain the warping of time and perception in humans, in what are broadly referred to as pacemaker-accumulation (PA) models.

The PA model breaks down temporality and apprehension into three phases. The first, the 'accumulation phase', begins when we encounter something and a switch in the brain is turned off, allowing the pulses of our internal clock to enter an accumulator. The number of pulses equates to the amount of time that we experience passing for that interval. Then the 'memory phase' begins, and the experience of the interval (described by the number of pulses accumulated) is transferred from the parts of the brain responsible for the working memory of the present moment, to those dealing with long-term memory. In the final 'decision-making' phase, we compare the duration of the recent interval with those stored in our long-term memory, which act as templates for reference. We then judge the length of the new experience according to this comparison, and so it seems to us either longer or shorter.

If encountering something new requires our brains to use more energy to apprehend it, then the neural activity increases, so both the novelty and level of attention will vary the timing of the switch being turned off and the rate of the pacemaker, which in turn creates a variance in the perceived duration of the new interval experienced. Put simply, the more novel the experience of the stimulus, the more pulses are accumulated during the interval, and the more slowly time will seem to pass.

*

There was a period when you were a baby, I don't remember how many months old, when you would cry if a stranger turned up at the house. It could be a friend or relative or parcel courier. Their appearance shocked and overwhelmed you. Worse was when a handful of people arrived all at once and we would hug and laugh and chat excitedly, like parrots squawking in a canopy. You hated that. We learned to introduce you slowly, but it didn't help much, and there was always a wobbly period of up to an hour when someone addressing you directly or leaning in too close would set you weeping. On one occasion, a friend leaned down and peered into your pushchair, and you screamed and wept so persistently that we had to send him away.

In particular, you hated laughing: the room erupting without warning, and you never in on the joke. How you must have felt the butt of it. How cruel it must have seemed, and in your own living room. As you got older we could better prepare you, warn you, tell you who was coming, show you pictures, extol the many virtues of our guests, explain that they had come to see you, to play with you, to bring you a present. It seemed to help, but once they arrived you would hide and peer at them, and we had to pretend we couldn't see you until your reconnaissance was complete.

It was a little embarrassing and frustrating, because we so wanted other people to know you the way we did, so confident and silly, and strong-willed, and not this small neurotic, crotchety recluse who forbade laughter in her company. I realise how unfair it was to expect anything else of you. Your days and nights were filled with routine and repetition, our voices, our laughter. Anyone else turning up at the door was an oddball item by default, slowing the world and throwing your apprehensive faculties wide open. In such a state of wild and permanent novelty you were so readily alert, your little internal clock accelerating its pulse, dopamine flooding the banks of your brain, your metabolism churning out calories of energy just to keep pace with all the neural activity fizzing in your skull, like an ice cube dropped in cola. For a two-year-old a year is half their life; what adventure was a day; what a vista a minute!

A roomful of strangers bursting out laughing must have been a grotesque, hyperreal tableau of teeth and gums, the black recesses of each mouth-hole enlarging, and the sound of it like bad piano, bad weather, iron machinery malfunctioning the air. Even that poor friend's darling face appearing beneath the awning of your buggy must have descended from the quiet periphery like a huge wax moon, gurning wide and stuffed with teeth. Who wouldn't wail, with these nightmares alive, and your parents waving them all across the threshold?

*

Daughter we are very vivid
for each other, slowing
a new word into the song.
In a rush for your survival
I let my love go by, no interval
to stave or demarcate
against the great compression.

Meet me regular now on this step
looking down at you, all grown,
your opinions shining like stones
held up fresh from a held-up river.
How can I stay jaded by the air
when you are here, breathing it

120

faster by default? I can't keep up
and won't, one day, you know.
That's exactly how I want it:
to lose my grip upon the now
and loom, and leave this present
all to you, my oddball,
most novel item, afford me
this pause for there is no
repetition and each leap is a new
leap, go on! Jump! I'll catch you.

VII.

MORE POETRY IN MONEY
THAN MONEY IN POETRY

When you were nearly two you started pulling out the big recycling boxes from the low shelf in the kitchen and setting up a shop. You didn't gather or display anything to sell, so we, as customers, had to invent your wares: a huge pair of trousers that we mimed trying on, a jelly we struggled with as it wobbled on its plate, a shoe so tiny we could barely pick it up, which we were always losing and finding again ... You happily took our imaginary money too, repeating the game over and over until – oh dear – there was nothing left to sell, thank goodness.

At Granny's house you went into the newspaper and cardboard ice cream business and, encouraged by your entrepreneurial spirit, we bought you a small wooden cash register for your birthday. It came with pretend coins and bills and a couple of laminated-paper debit cards. We taught you how to scan items by passing them over the top of the till, and you learned to make the *beep* yourself. But you always struggled with the money side of things. Your mum taught you, adorably, to ask us whether we would be paying by cash or by card, but this was a kind of floating utterance that didn't correspond to any subsequent action.

We would put our items (your toys) into our bag and then make to leave, but you would inevitably try and give us some money as well, and when we tried to give you the money back you would put it into our shopping bag. The monetary transaction did not need to happen in a particular order or correspond to any sense of value or exchange, so long as it had all the constituent parts. It was a kind of situationist, deconstructed shopping experience, prioritising the social codes and mannerism of shopping over the specific functionality of its structures, which was of little or no concern. Absolute chaos. I enjoyed it.

Now you know that we exchange money for things in shops, but you have no sense of what happens beyond that singular transaction; the money goes into the till and its story ends there. I feel an urge to protect you from the further story of money, where it comes from, where it goes . . . It is such a terrifying form of metaphor, rigged in one direction. Monetary value asserts an object's transcendence beyond its material properties, into a realm of free exchange, but this happens only by replacing the object with a transactable emptiness; its discrete qualities must be factored out, extracted, so that it answers to a sleek, new, numerical name. Efficiency by reduction. A brute form of symbolism, which tenderises and dissolves all that it encounters so that it might pass through the nozzle and disappear into the machinery of atomisation and abstract potential.

Monetary value only exists in the human mind. Our bodies and the work that they do, and all the experiences that we accrue when we are doing it, must be left behind, as collateral for the free play of the system of exchange. You do something for money, and it is worth the money you get for it, and according to money the rest is sentimental, remainder, leftovers. It is a kind of intellectual disfiguring, a religion of liquidity; monetary value wants all things molten, pulped and transmissible. What, in the end, can't be sold? Bodily organs, landmines, undrilled oil, children taken from one car to another ... that is the story of where money goes and where it comes from. It is a translator of pure abstraction, blameless and naïve to the handshakes in the boardroom and the lobby and the lay-by. Money is oblique by definition. It won't be there ... it only ever happens nearby.

For someone to have money, somebody else, somewhere, has to have no money at all. It does not seem that way, but it's true. How else could a penny be worth slightly more than nothing? You have to have *no money* so that *some money* can be more. Money relies entirely on that exclusion. I, like most people in the UK, have less than no money nearly all the time. It does not seem that way, but it's true. There are overdrafts, there are credit-card debts and student loans and bank loans and mortgages ... cold, real, but not quite solid.

According to the Office for National Statistics,

Total household debt in Great Britain was £1.28 trillion in April 2016 to March 2018.

That is comfortably more than half of our GDP, while also being part of it. That should not surprise us, because money is debt. That's what happens when you rig a metaphor in one direction. A banknote is literally a promissory IOU. It says so on one side:

I promise to pay the bearer on demand the sum of [twenty] pounds. [signed] London, for the Governor and Company of the Bank of England, Sarah John, Chief Cashier.

If you don't have any hard cash, any promissory items of currency, then you may have money in your bank account, which you can also demand to be paid 'the sum of'. British banks evolved from goldsmiths. In the seventeenth century, they would lend money on the security of gold and precious items that they stored safely for their customers. Now there is no actual gold in the bank, just notes referring to numbers, floating, like intent, like motive ... So money relies on trust and faith. If you can't inspire enough faith that you will make good on the promise, if you can't be trusted that you are 'good for your money', then a bank will not loan you money, will not allow you to be indebted, will not grant you credit, will not give you the option of having *less than no money*. Having *less than no money* in this system is better than having *no money* because credit, inspired by faith, can be spent, whereas *no money* cannot. How can someone who has *less than no money* have more money to spend than someone who only has *no money*? Because the faith you inspire in those to whom you might be indebted is worth more than the money you actually have, because money is only the promise of a debt being one day repaid: money is the faith you inspire. If you are already rich you can inspire faith more easily.

And what if you cannot inspire any faith, or pay your debts? What if you have no money? Well, then you are excluded from anything that money can potentially become, and anything that can potentially become money. Anything is potentially everything.

*

A 2003 functional MRI (fMRI) study led by Naomi Eisenberger, professor of psychology at UCLA, showed that the same neural regions of the brain engaged by social exclusion were also engaged by the experience of physical pain. Participants in the study were monitored while first playing, and then being excluded from, a simple ball-tossing game, and fMRI scans showed that the anterior cingulate region of the brain was more active when they were excluded from the game, and made to watch. This correlated almost exactly with data collected from previous studies of the experience of physical pain.

*

Today I gave you a shiny ten-pence piece that you treasure and carry around and enjoy posting down the gaps in the radiators or forcing into the keyholes of the doors upstairs. This does not inspire faith. When the coin gets stuck I refuse to give you another one. You cry.

*

In 2008, three Japanese neurologists conducted a study in which an fMRI scanner monitored the blood flow in the brains of participants who were rewarded money while playing a simple gambling game. The results showed that the higher the reward, the higher the participants' neural activity in an area of the brain known as the striatum, as well as in the orbitofrontal cortex and the insula. On the second day of the study, instead of receiving money the participants were rewarded with positive feedback about their personalities: they were shown love. The team concluded that there was a

> substantial overlap between the neural representation of monetary and social reward. In particular, the left putamen and caudate nucleus showed greater activity in response to both higher monetary payoffs and more positive evaluations of the self.

*

Social reward (love) is processed in the brain as if it were money (love).

(love)   (love)

The withdrawal of money (love) is an exclusion from the system of

(love)

social reward (love).

(love)

Social exclusion ~~(money)~~ is experienced in the brain as if it
            (money)

were pain ~~(pain)~~.
    (pain)

To have money ~~(love)~~ is to process social reward ~~(love)~~ by entering
         (love)   (love)

into systemic complicity in the exclusion ~~(pain)~~ of another person
                (pain)

from ~~(love)~~ the social system of reward ~~(money)~~ in a way that the
   (love)   (money)

person will process in the brain ~~(pain)~~ as if it were physical pain ~~(pain)~~.
        (pain)   (pain)

*

> *Who is that?*
> It's the Queen.
> *The Queen?*
> Yes, the Queen of England and … other places.
> *England?*
> Yes, she's the head of state … it's complicated
> … don't worry about it.
> *Why is the Queen on the money?*
> That's a good question.

*

In her book *Virtue, Fortune and Faith: A Genealogy of Finance*, the political scientist Marieke de Goede provides a brilliant analysis of finance and its practices, demonstrating 'the inextricability of money and representation' and showing how it is held up by all kinds of uncertain symbols, culturally produced suppositions and moral assumptions. She argues that,

> financial instruments and practices are discursively constituted and firmly rooted in cultural, moral, political, and religious

127

history. A closer look at money and credit makes it impossible to abstract them from practices of representation.

She continues:

> The issue of reality and representation – of 'real' value embodied by gold versus intangible faith in paper money [...] is at the heart of contemporary financial practices [...] some early banknotes actually depicted the coins of gold or silver that they could be redeemed for. But more often, banknotes generate faith by depicting authority in a different way.

We encounter these depictions of authority in our own money today: heads of state, prominent buildings, insignia, 'In God We Trust' on the twenty-dollar bill, or Churchill's weird words on the five-pound note: 'I have nothing to offer but blood, toil, tears and sweat.'

The symbols on banknotes are not just commemorative or celebratory images drawn from a supposedly common national heritage, they are designed to call upon the authority that their symbols depict in order to authenticate the currency, to symbolise the power by which its value is assured. They are supposed to be a threat to those that would question the validity of that value; they are articles designed to inspire faith among the faithful, or else enforce that faith among any doubters. As De Goede puts it:

> The imagery on paper banknotes does not just *aid* the representation of value but comes to *generate* this value itself.

Money relies on imagery: that sensory, connotative, uncertain stuff of poetry and poetics. How often have you heard people referring to foreign currency playfully as 'toy money' because of the novelty of its images? When the leader depicted is not our leader, how can they inspire fear or submission? As De Goede argues, they do this because finance is a

discursive domain made possible through performative practices, which have to be articulated and rearticulated on a daily basis.

To believe a currency, you have to have been part of this communal performance, through countless daily exchanges, until its symbolic authority has been sufficiently articulated and rearticulated. Learning the language of foreign money is just like practising from a phrasebook: by the end of your holiday you have rearticulated the authority of foreign banknote imagery many times, just as you have rearticulated those awkward new syllables: combien, cuanta, quanto, kolko, koliko, immisa, ikura, eolmayeyo, elo ni, hur mycket, sakumaha, vi fil, wie viel ... Money gains its authority through repetition, just as any word reproduces its meaning through repetition in endless new contexts.

*

At the time of writing there are 1,912 five-pound notes in circulation. It is the rarest note. The next rarest is the ten-pound note, of which there are 8,006, then comes the twenty-pound note, the most common one, of which there are 43,357. There are 15,651 fifty-pound notes in circulation. Fifty-*one*. I wonder who has it, that last fifty-pound note. No one I hang out with, that's for sure. It must be out there, though, otherwise how can the bank know exactly how much faith has been created?

You cannot have faith without its opposite. Faith implies doubt, includes it, in order to sustain itself. So money must include doubt too.

We hear about uncertainty in relation to money all the time.

129

Uncertainty is bad for businesses and bad for speculation and growth, because uncertainty is risk. But uncertainty is good for marketeers, who trade in promises, and who need risk, fluctuations, booms and busts to be able to go in low in the hope of coming out high. A static market is hardly a market at all; the value of money, like an electron, is only *there* when it changes its state, moving from probability into a fixed, or measurable, or quantifiable position. The economy does seem a bit like the quantum world, with its weather system of probabilities, its awareness of how observers 'spook' and inflect upon the observed, and its reliance on symbolic manoeuvres of uncertain computation that describe a reality one can never encounter, always at one remove.

This is not a new observation: traders have been using quantum mathematics to calculate market probabilities for over a decade. There are several books written by those who made millions from it.

*

That love and money aren't that different for the brain should be obvious, because they are not so different. I do not mean to be provocatively unromantic by making this statement. Quite the opposite. What I mean is, that money is not really separate from the rest of human life. Indebtedness, reimbursement, speculation, investment, are just cold, reductive terminology for the complex range of social operations that we use to organise and understand our relationships with one another, and they far predate the symbolic realm of currency and monetary exchange.

> Swap me a year in love for a glass
> of cold water, this watermelon
> for the hat you wore that day
> ... OK, now tell me what being

alive is like for you and I will

cut your sister's hair.

Love and money are both kept afloat by our participation and renewed vows of agreement. Or, as De Goede writes about finance, they are 'performative practices, which have to be articulated and rearticulated'. The difference is in the policing of terms, for the faith that money creates only has to be named numerically. The reality that money is a human language must be strenuously denied for the preservation of the system's purity and undeniability of value. And yet, ownership, as an idea, is deeply sentimental; the concept of abstract value is a giddying romance; exact exchange is a passionate fantasy; speculation and risk are hot and pliable yearnings, money is a breathy, touchy, frictional group activity ... There's no such thing as cold, hard cash; cash is erogenous. It needs us to exchange, to swap, to want and desire it: it needs our bodies.

*

In 1971, Richard Nixon decided to effectively end the so-called Bretton Woods system, which since 1958 had fixed the value of the forty-four participating countries' currencies to the US dollar, with only the dollar being fixed directly to the price of gold. At the time, the US owned three quarters of global gold reserves, its economy was huge, and its goods and services in demand worldwide, as other nations recovered from war. To have the US economy as the central tent pole made perfect sense. By the 1960s, however, as exports from the UK, Europe and Japan became more competitive, the dollar became less desirable than the gold it might be traded for. By 1971, with inflation rising at home, and in a bid to stop everyone cashing in their dollars for US gold stock, Nixon decided to free the dollar from the gold standard. By 1973, the relatively free global trading of international currencies we see in today's foreign exchange markets began in earnest.

Just as Newtonian physics was replaced by the new, uncertain mathematical languages of quantum mechanics and the general theory of relativity, so the dollar was freed from its material equivalent, and money could wander and figure in purely mathematical terms. Only it didn't. In 1974, Nixon agreed with King Faisal of Saudi Arabia to set oil prices in US dollars, meaning that any country wanting to purchase Saudi oil would first have convert its currency into dollars. The so-called petrodollar was born, with other oil-exporting countries following suit and pricing their oil in US dollars.

The enormous sums that the Saudi government made through its oil exports created more wealth than could be efficiently reinvested into the Saudi economy, with its relatively small population. Part of the secret terms of this new petrodollar system was an agreement that these surpluses would be used for the large-scale purchase of US bonds and treasury bills, in a process known as recycling. Petrodollar recycling would also be underpinned by the promise of US military protection and collaboration, along with large military contracts. This deal has helped create enormous liquidity for US markets, but over time it also meant that Saudi Arabia has effectively become one of the US Government's largest foreign creditors. After decades of secrecy around the 1974 deal and its financial legacy it was finally revealed in 2016 that Saudi Arabia had $117 billion invested in US government debt, though the actual figure is thought to be much higher.

The scale of the US debt makes the military underpinning of the petrodollar system interesting. It is a stark example of the value of the dollar being upheld by the threat of violence. That Saddam Hussein made the decision to trade oil in euros in

October 2001 has been cited as a significant contributing factor in the US's decision to invade the country a year and a half later. US military dominance and its monetary hegemony are intrinsically linked, in just the same way as the symbols of authority can be said to support and uphold the value of a banknote.

*

The philosopher Franco 'Bifo' Berardi argues that economists

> should not even be considered scientists. They are much more similar to priests [...] [they] are beset with dogmatic notions like growth, competition, and gross national product, and they determine that social reality is out of order when it is not matching these criteria.

It is a damning indictment, though surely a generalisation. Given how enormous a trust we place in 'economic science' to interpret the behaviour of markets, it seems vital that, rather than accept the seemingly scientific methodology of our financial institutions, we also try to understand the performative practices of authentication at work within them, and where they derive their authority from, given that their facts and figures are, in fact, more figurative than factual. De Goede is less rhetorical and sweeping than Berardi in her assessment, but she is firmly sceptical about the supposedly moral, rational motives of the scientists who study and legitimise financial practices:

> They determine what it is possible to speak of within the historically constituted financial sphere, which events are recorded as evidence and which utterances are recognized as valid. [...] Indeed, is it not precisely through its *exclusions* that a more or less coherent financial domain becomes thinkable at all?

It is clear that economics can only offer a highly limited description of the world. The primacy it has is upheld with power in mind, and not human well-being or environmental sustainability. It is also underwritten by violence, be it military violence on a global scale or the threat of social exclusion and poverty on an individual level. No science can treat the errant, wavering and improbable business of human life as an inconvenient secondary sphere of reality. A science of economics needs to be more inclusive, more aware of the uncertain and intersubjective nature of its knowledge-claims. As De Goede puts it:

> Precisely because it is based on faith and confidence, the functioning of money and finance requires strong nodal points of (discursive) authority supporting and maintaining that faith.

Just as Lorraine Code dismantles the idealised 'masculine' notion of an autonomous knowledge that supposedly 'transcends experience', De Goede also demonstrates how finance is produced by similar masculine idealisations. She charts the sexualised representations of 'Lady Credit' in eighteenth-century political discourse, as well as earlier instances, where

> the desirable and seductive wealth of speculation became represented by images of women and goddesses, frequently of loose sexual morals.

Modern finance has inherited these eighteenth-century masculine, idealised notions of mastery, resisting temptation, the gentlemanly code and self-control, but these ideals do not stand up to scrutiny. Greed and power are not monastically forbidden or met with abstention, but tolerated, renamed, denied and hidden from view. The crash in 2008 was not caused by a small number of callous maverick gamblers infiltrating an otherwise clean and proper system, it was the result of 'morally hazardous' behaviours within companies and institutions that considered themselves 'too big to fail'. The knowledge that they were so existentially entrenched in and integral to the national and global economies gave these companies the confidence to take risks they could not conceivably countenance on their own. We continue to tolerate the bailouts, the enforced public crutches and stanchions erected to protect this system, in the casual belief that the system is founded on sound and certain thinking and behaviour. If enough of us benefit … If it works most of the time … If I can still have *less than no money* … In reality, it is *our* faith that created the financial institutions. It amazes me that such faith has not yet run its course, because when we mistake the power of finance for certainty in its workings, then we only hand it more power, more confidence, and so permit it to act less and less reasonably. If we continue to democratically return governments whose personnel either is invested in these same institutions or might be courted by their lobbyists, or whose own party depends on donations from financial institutions, then we should be asking more loudly and consistently how easily and willingly our state funds might be used as collateral, as insurance against the financial risks being taken by these private operators.

*

I look at the word 'love', like an apple bobbing in a barrel. Or like a plump little doughnut, leaking jam from a bruise on its side, where the waistband of dough is lighter, more vulnerable. Love itself is dynamic, various, technical, expansive, capacious, infinitesimal, but the word 'love', now I look again, is wet wood, tired pet, waiting-room smell, and car-park area. 'Love', oh earthly signage propped against the wall. 'Love', oh veteran horse of the burnished prairies: no synonym, no understudy, the moon on your back on your constant commute. I feel sorry for you, 'love'. But God, do I love. I am pathetic with it. Blowsy and eager and saturated, left out like cotton sheets in cotton sheets of rain.

The striatum, and the orbitofrontal cortex, and the insula can do what they want, but money is not like love. Money is a toy. Love is ... *How many times has the bucket been sent down this well, poet?* Not enough times yet! Love is hydrogen. Love is a cough in the hedge. Love is procrastination over the act of dying. Love is marsupial and sexy on a hinge. Give it what it wants. Tender its direction with a wet thumb and a savings account. Put it in your mouth, for God's sake. Put your thumb in the pie and pop out the plum. Nothing else for me. I'm cooked on both sides, I'm done. I love you. I love you. I love you.

In her brilliant and restorative lecture for the British Academy, 'The Determination of Love', the poet Andrea Brady writes:

'I love you' is simultaneously the most powerful and direct expression of love, and its most inadequate shadow; it is necessary, singular, and powerful, but also repetitive – not only of all the times you've said it yourself, to different people, in different situations, but also of the whole history of human love.

I do not leave the house without saying it, like a hex.

'I love you' relies on its rearticulation too, and not just by saying it occasionally, but by performing the full gambit of our daily practices in its honour. A vow, confession or promise is useless if it is not backed up by the behaviour that continually renews it. You must remake the beds you choose to lie in, in love, and that passionate resource of mundane energy reclaims the word, mints its endless variousness, reproducing love each time, embossed with a new definition.

It is for this reason that poems make such suitable homes for

136

love, as each new reader and reading allows for love's recontextualising. Poems are where I find love most commonly presented in its uncertain complexity, because the language of metaphor and connotation ask us to be active in bringing our loves to bear upon the love we find described. It's in poems that I am best invited to be a participant in other loves, to illuminate by my love their geodic interiors, and find the contractual specifics. For all the cliché and repetition of courtly tropes, those gaudy, cheesy, swooning, sashaying endings, the recalibration of my love by love poetry fills my future anew with love's possibility.

A lot of people are annoyed by Shakespeare's famous ending to Sonnet 18:

> But thy eternal summer shall not fade
> Nor lose possession of that fair thou ow'st,
> Nor shall death brag thou wander'st in his shade
> When in eternal lines to time thou grow'st.
>   So long as men can breathe or eyes can see,
>   So long lives this, and this gives life to thee.

The poor addressee is outlived by the poem, and the author, by his virtuosity, is the real star of the show, its real subject. I can take that view: Shakespeare waving his sonneteering prowess around, a smooth, virtuoso fuckboy, gunning for his place in eternity, his lover written over, his love besides the point, his poem really, really good ... But he's also right, isn't he. The lover is still here, whoever they were, wandering just beyond the shade of death; I'd be happy with that. He didn't know it would happen, he wished it for them, he chanced that hope, as an in-joke between them. Only a poem, after all. Only fourteen lines to fight the rest of time, to survive all intervening events and bring them here before us, more temperate and lovely than a day in summer. He refuses to accept their death, he refuses it. That's not showing off. That's desperate, and sad in its futility. No wonder we keep this hopeful charm in print. It's our own sad and futile plea. Our dark little in-joke, which we sleep beside, and worry about and rearticulate into currency more than anything else. Please.

So long lives this, and this gives life to thee.

*

I don't remember when it happened, or how old you were, I think maybe nineteen or twenty months, but we were walking up the driveway from the gallery and arts centre in the middle of town, where we'd been killing time in the café waiting for the worst of the rain to stop. We had the buggy, but you wanted to be carried, so I was steering it awkwardly with one hand while you played with my ear and the hair around it, tugging occasionally, as a game, to get a reaction. I was telling you about what we were going to do when we got home. I promised to make you a chocolate milkshake – which is really just almond milk with a teaspoon of cocoa powder, that I shake in your cup until it all goes brown – and after discussing what might be on television we fell into a short silence. Then, for the first time, unprompted, as a thought occurring first in your own unfathomable head, a shimmer of electricity finding a route through your brain, landing in the place where words arrive, you said,

I love you, Daddy.

And I said, *I love you too.* And the rain started to get heavier again, and you let me put you in the buggy, and fuss the rain cover over you, and I put my hood up and started walking, without a single articulatable thought in my whole fucking head for the ten minutes it took us to get from that place to our front door.

138

VIII.

SILLINESS AND INTIMACY

You are a deeply silly person. I am so pleased. Welcome. We can all be chickens. We can all pull our trousers right up and strut. The hard work of getting you to stop, calm down, listen, be good, see danger where we see danger, is done for the day, and now this silliness is our harbour, where we can locate each other again. Thank God. I am so tired of teaching you *not* to do things. Some days it seems as if all I have done is snap at you, get at you, let my impatience with your inexperience overwhelm me. It took an hour to get your shoes and socks on and you out of the house and in the shop you refused to stay in your buggy, growing angry and upset, and when I caved in and let you out, just to avoid a scene, you grabbed at shelves, tins and jars, your hands, grubby from the park, roaming over the vegetables, the fruit, and then you took a bite from the side of a pineapple while I was getting bananas, so I had to fucking buy it, this huge fruit with its ridiculous hairdo too big for my basket. I placated you with a lurid magazine, with its free plastic shit destined for landfill, but I didn't care, I needed to get home to make dinner, I needed to get home, through the rain, it was autumn and cold, I needed to get home so I could stick you in front of a brightly lit screen, so I could chop an onion without being disturbed, so I could have a train of thought to myself for just five fucking minutes, and then suddenly you wailed and wailed from the other room, so I ran to you, I dropped the knife on the sideboard and ran in a panic but all you had done, ragged and tired, was stand on the television remote and switch to BBC News 24, so I grabbed the remote to change it back to your cartoon, but every stage of the way, every button I pressed – to bring up the Home screen, to bring up the Apps screen, to select the Continue Watching tab, to select the Resume option – you continued yelling, *No, not that! No, that's not it! Not that one!*, until I shouted *I'M DOING IT FOR FUCK'S SAKE JUST WAIT WILL YOU!* my rage like a bag of blood giving way, the guilt instant, the shock on your face . . . my juror, sweet little pineapple biter, I am not like that, I promise. I am silly.

I even said it,

Silly daddy. I shouldn't have shouted.

And I let you say it too,

Silly daddy,

so then I head back to the kitchen, my apologies tendered, my tenderness assured, my remorse like roadkill that I prod at and turn over in my mind as I stir the wooden spoon as long as I can bear before folding, and turning from the stove, my hands over my face, my forehead against the fridge now, letting out the sigh I needed. Then the second sigh I needed even more. Then the third long sigh that I must have gathered up inside me earlier . . . maybe in the park with the dog off its lead coming close, boldly, or on the narrow pavement, the van doing 60 down our narrow 30 street, when I muttered *prick* instead of screaming it

140

like I wanted to. Maybe that was the third sigh, the remainder carried over, the slag from the ore, and then you're back there, in the doorway,

> *Daddy can I have something to drink?*
> Of course you can, my love.

Kneeling down to hand you the cup, pushing back your fringe behind your ear, it's not your fault, it's my fault, my eyes filling at the edges.

> There you go.

It is so fucking hard. And I am not a bad person. Please understand. I know that anger and remorse are a noxious pattern. We both have our limits, and I try, I really fucking try. So you see, it is important that after all that, all the terseness and the stress, that you watch me take these long strides across the room, with my index fingers pointing out from my chest for nipple-antennae, with my nostrils flared, and my eyes crossed; it matters to me that I do a stance and say, *What you think about this stance? You try. Fantastic!* So please do jump off the sofa onto the cushions, shouting *panks!* whatever that means, and do wiggle your bum and laugh at me laughing. Maybe in all the excitement you'll let out a fart. Bravo! Not bad for an involuntary one. You have twenty minutes before bath time, and I am so tired of being stern and alert and afraid on your behalf. Life is here, in all directions. So feast, you daft little cherub. There is practically nothing in life better than being incredibly silly, and I will not deny you, I refuse to deny you. This is our valve, your hand is on the faucet.

*

141

Playfulness is not silliness. When we play there is a discernible purpose, a reason. The cat is going down the slide. The dinosaur is scared, so we must make him a den under the table. We animate your toys according to your experiences and your understanding of those experiences. In doing so, we investigate and advance the limits of that understanding. Play is experimentation, and a kind of training – a scaled down arena in which to exact and enact fundamental relations, social, linguistic, but also physical and material: ladders, puzzles, Duplo, containers and connectors ... Play is a serious business upon which your mind and your survival will depend. These are your furrows and footpaths: we are treading them down in advance, we are rehearsing in code.

Silliness does not adhere to reason. The slide goes down the cat. The law is a headwind, so in silliness we tack. Let us find things to do by doing them. Where does the body want to bend? Silliness is a language of radical, directionless extremity, a scrambling of the seams. Like Deleuze and Guattari's rhizomes, those 'deterritorialized lines of desire', silliness locates points of porosity, or wires up an error into light. It refutes consequence, since no outcome is sought in meaning, what happens is only silly. Like Mikhail Bakhtin's 'carnivalistic *mésalliances*', in silliness the certain echelons and opposites dissolve, Heaven and Hell are reunited and the beggar shits on the cloak of the king who vomits coins into a vase of fire. My authority, flimsy though it is, defiant though you are, is relinquished. There is nothing to fear, no system to fail by. I have taken it away so that you can see me. Really see me. Silliness is intimacy.

I remember years ago, before you were born, I tried out my theory of silliness as intimacy on a few friends. They all agreed: the people they were close to were the people they were silliest with. Not always, but correlation enough for my hypothesis. One friend told me how her father, a stern man, reserved and quiet, respected, perhaps even a little feared in the town where he lived, used to heave up his trousers to just below the nipple, and swagger around, drawling a Farmer John voice for their amusement. She recalled how shocking it was to see him lighten himself like that, compared to the man they observed in the world. The walls collapsing, the burden of being who he was disbanded, written off. Then, later, when her visa ran out and she returned to the States, I saw a post on her Instagram account, saying that her father had died. It had happened quite suddenly, though they'd had time to say their goodbyes. And I looked at the pictures she put up, and in each he was smiling, horsing around. Those were the images she wanted to show us, that she felt conveyed him best. I want to be remembered at my silliest. How true we are then. How close.

*

Silliness can be a way of sounding people out. You can't always expect it right away, because silliness, intimacy, can be costly: it is a vulnerable stance. In the French region of Franche-Comté, when they make Comté cheese, they store the wheels for months in large cellars. A 'jury terroir' of specialist cheese inspectors goes around to verify the produce, and one of the tests, for ripeness, involves tapping on the cheese with a little hammer. I don't know what sound they are looking for. I don't know anything more about it. But when I think about trying to find silliness among adults, I think about the hammer on the side of the cheese. Tap tap. Are you ripe? Are you ready?

*

I was once at a party with lots of people I didn't know. The host introduced me to a man who had just arrived with a carrier bag full of bottles of beer. He offered me one politely, and by the time I looked up the host had been drawn away elsewhere, and we, two strangers with our unopened bottles, were left to fend for ourselves. I took out a cigarette lighter from my pocket to lever off the bottle caps, and he gestured *you go first* with his eyebrows and eyes, so I opened the beer he had kindly donated and, then (tap tap on the side of his cheese) I passed him not the lighter to open his own, but the bottle top. I don't know why I did it. It was a bit of a gamble. A bit annoying, but it was, I sensed, also an opportunity, an opening. *Ah thanks!* He said. *I'll put that in my lid room.* And we laughed as I then passed him the lighter. I won't bore you with the whole conversation, how far we travelled in silliness, his favourite lid, the lid conventions he goes to every month . . . you can imagine. But when we were joined by another of his friends, she assumed we had known one another for years.

I have always been grateful for silliness among men. Like a handshake or a code word, silliness and its invitation to intimacy allows us to soften ourselves, particularly if we are strangers. Within silliness there is not much room for rutting, for the coded, bristling forms of toxic masculine competition. It relies instead on collaboration, on exploring possible silly avenues together, in a kind of mutual steering. It can be tender, to read each other that way, and since it's fun, the goal is our mutual pleasure. At times you can find yourself in a race to be the funniest, which kills the joy. It is the benign, creative form of silliness I seek. I have found the most lovely men I know by being silly with them. I sense that we treasure one another for it. It is such a relief, and relief – did I mention? – is my favourite emotion.

I am not saying at all that silliness is a masculine domain. Your mother is possibly the silliest person I know, and in accordance with my theory, she is also the person I know most intimately, and who I love with a totality I cannot find the edges of. I know many, many women and non-binary people who laugh like barns from silliness, and they would probably remind me that the social costs of silliness for people who are not men are higher. They

144

would remind me that for all the joy of the intimacy between men achieved through silliness, there are lots of people who first have to fight to be taken seriously.

*

I was speaking to my friend Theis about silliness and intimacy, and it turned out they had researched and written about the word 'silly' with regards to etymological drift and the phenomenon of 'semantic degeneration': when a word cedes its positive associations to negative ones. Theis explained that the Middle English *sely* or *seely* meant something more like 'deserving of pity', perhaps referring to the ailing or frail. But it was also widely used to mean 'harmless' and 'benign', and also 'happy' or 'lucky'. It is only later that the negative associations became more predominant: 'lacking in judgement or common sense', 'foolishness' or 'stupidity', 'empty-headedness'. That drift from harmlessness to foolishness feels so tragic to me: you cannot help but read the later definition as an indictment of the qualities of the earlier one. Is it too much of a leap to infer that violence, power and judiciousness have become married concepts; that weakness has come to be seen as irrational? The fetish of pure reason, those idealised masculine obelisks ... doesn't that appetite for certainty require the violent erasure of that which is deemed irrational from the category of knowledge? Is it not in fact irrational to desire a world without silliness? And surely it is violent too, to seek to deny the intimacy that silliness affords us.

It is the ultra-rationalists who are seely, deserving of pity, and, yes, foolish too. I almost feel sorry for them.

*

O pity me, my mind is sick
and lucky. Bring me your groceries
drooled on and overtouched
and I will struggle to return them

to the aisle of category and reason,
but keep your teeth-marks
in the side of a pineapple,
and the pineapple too, foolish
irrational thing. Irrational rain
drifting, autumn degenerating:
why do fools
love in fall?
Tap tap. Tap tap.
On the side of our life
ripening to a pitch discernible
only to a specialist like you,
my juror, my three long sighs
paid out, I am tired
of being afraid. Let's go home.

IX.

A HOME IN UNCERTAINTY

The term 'scepticism' derives from *skepsis*, the Greek word for examination or enquiry. Scepticism is taking a humble stance on the truth, founded on an acknowledgement of our epistemic limitations. But it carries more pejorative connotations too. While it is generally accepted that everyone is entitled to interrogate a thesis before deciding where they stand based on the evidence provided, the sceptic is characterised by their persistent diligence in proving *beyond doubt* during the process of truth-making. They *remain* sceptical, because the truth of the matter (perhaps any matter at all) is itself unreasonable as an absolute claim. How we view scepticism, and the sceptic as an individual, is really a judgement, then, on how much doubt we find reasonable and for how long. The sceptic's acceptance is always pending, they seek to prolong the arrival of truth indefinitely; nothing can be finalised. Their unreasonable demand for absolute evidence (which they know cannot be met, otherwise they would not be sceptics) means they have chosen the path of the obstacle, to be obtuse to knowledge: distrusting, agnostic refuseniks, epistemic hand-wringers, thorny sticks-in-the-mud, attention-seekers, stubborn, nihilistic brain-haters – there's always a problem, there's always a further condition to be met, there's always bloody one, isn't there. Why can't you just accept it, if it's workable, practical, easy? It's good enough for most people, why do you have to be different? Why make it all about you?

I don't know what the truth is. I think anyone who claims to know the absolute truth about anything is a fucking liar, because knowledge and truth have to be two different things; I cannot see or conceive of it otherwise. In my mind, I occupy two houses: First, a house of knowledge, which is tenuous, mutable, human, beautiful, difficult, provisional, limited, built, languagey, dangerous, renegotiable, political and socialised ... I can dream of it, I can lick it, and lean upon its walls. Then I keep a house of truth, which I never go to, because I don't know where it is or how I would ever find it except by accepting that it is not there, that its threshold recedes from my steps in the dark, that its deeds cannot bear my name ... that house of singularity ... I have given up, the truest thing I ever did.

I don't know how to tell you. That there is all of this ... rigging, this ergonomic, sensuous extension of yourself, by which you will forbear and witness your being alive, and then there is everything else that exists according to the ways you cannot know, name or reach. You get to keep this static wind, this thawing-out of time around you, and all the delicate categories you can rub against and decorate with your intellect, and by God, knowledge is enough for one person and a lifetime, but there is also the truth, your face always up against the door, the door that is the edge of yourself and the time you have inside of it. I can keep it from you, the only truth I know. You're only three, yesterday, your candles and cake, and it's only one lie, the two houses.

But there will be a day for your first sip of honesty. Thereafter, increments and mishaps of grief and realisation. It's so beautiful: to be outmanoeuvred by the truth. I'm almost excited.

*

The large body of philosophical works categorised as 'ancient scepticism' can be roughly divided into 'Pyrrhonian scepticism', named after Pyrrho of Elis, and the 'academic sceptics', who operated out of Plato's academy, albeit some seventy-five years after his death. Taking from Plato's dialogues that *nothing can be known with any certainty*, Arcesilaus of Pitane, the academy's sixth head, oversaw various innovations in sceptic thought that led to its growth into a major philosophical movement. One of the key aims of the early ancient sceptics was to disprove current dogmas, mainly those espoused by the Stoic philosophers.

The Stoics believed that knowledge can be apprehended by the mind via the human senses, and that the universe is governed by an absolute law. In order to categorise reality into that which is true and untrue, a Stoic sage enacted a process called *katalepsis*. Harald Thorsrud defines *katalepsis* as

> a mental grasping of a sense impression that guarantees the truth of what is grasped. If one assents to the proposition associated with a kataleptic impression, i.e. if one experiences katalepsis, then the associated proposition cannot fail to be true. The Stoic sage, as the perfection and fulfilment of human nature, is the one who assents only to kataleptic impressions and thus is infallible.

The stoics never suggested that anyone had achieved such a state of 'perfection and fulfilment', but Stoicism's founding philosopher, Zeno, nevertheless claimed the possibility of absolute truth in knowledge, and that he could give a correct account of what it was.

It was Carneades of Cyrene, a later head of Plato's academy

who made the famous claim that 'nothing can be known; not even this', who moved beyond disproving the positions asserted and defended by the Stoics into a broader critique of knowledge and truth. Carneades is particularly remarkable for his philosophical technique. He would argue vigorously for and against every argument to such a thorough and committed extent that people were often confused about which side of any given debate he was on. They were right to be confused. His aim was to effectively prove all arguments both right and wrong enough that no certain conclusion could be drawn, which was itself the only final conclusion.

Pyrrho was a poet, though none of his writing has survived. His philosophical doctrines are only recorded in fragments of writing by Timon of Phlius, one of Pyrrho's pupils, so very little is known about Pyrrho's actual beliefs. Pyrrho was a philosopher at the court of Alexander the Great and accompanied him on his conquest of India, where it is thought he spent time with the gymnosophist sect. Though the biographer Antigonus of Carystus is often cited, his accounts of Pyrrho's character are not regarded as reliable, mainly because Antigonus was not himself a philosopher. His anecdotes are intriguing, however. Pyrrho was said to have distrusted his senses to the extent that friends had to save him from walking off cliff edges and into busy roads. He is also said to have ignored many social norms of the day, cleaning his own house and even washing a pig. Another story has him remain perfectly calm during a storm at sea, pointing to a pig eating away on deck, oblivious to the danger, telling his distressed company that a wise man should exhibit the same behaviour.

What we know of Pyrrhonism as sceptic movement largely derives from the writings of Sextus Empiricus, in particular his book *Outlines of Pyrrhonism*, written some four-hundred years after Pyrrho's death. As well as preserving Timon's crucial fragments, Sextus develops a fuller account of Pyrrhonism as a belief system. Critical of the academic sceptics, whose denial of the possibility of knowledge Sextus regarded as dogmatic, Sextus instead believed that one should abstain from final judgement in all matters of knowledge and commit to a practice called *epoché*. One can still live habitually, and perceive and report on one's experience of reality according to one's senses, but such perceptions and reports are precisely that, and do not make the world more knowable in an objective, external way. A sceptic might also hold beliefs according to what they perceive as virtue, or in accordance with societal custom, but only so long as they recognise that such beliefs are in fact untrue according to the rigours and rules of philosophy and reason; a sceptic may opt to hold untrue beliefs, while remaining sceptical. Sextus did not find these ideas contradictory or impractical, but rather argued that, by always deferring belief and knowledge, one could achieve a state of *ataraxia*, of equanimity or imperturbability. Sextus argued that when one gives up on the burden of final judgement, tranquillity follows, just as the shadow follows the body.

*

The virus arrived in the UK at the end of January. By 7 March there were over two hundred confirmed cases. You came down with it a week later. There was no testing available, so we couldn't be sure. No one we knew had the virus yet, but we supposed it was at least *possible* that it might find us here, in Colchester. After all, this was a global pandemic, and it seemed to be getting fully underway. I was scared. You had a cough at night, and a temperature that soared and settled according to the four-hour cycle of your maximum Calpol dose. Your tonsils were covered in white spots and it hurt you to eat and drink. It lasted about seventy-two hours, and then you were fine.

Your mother came down with a fever a week later. It hit her

suddenly one evening, the night before Mother's Day, which she spent on the sofa under a blanket, weary and weak. The fever passed, but she developed an unusual shortness of breath, a pressure in her chest, which lasted five or six days. This was different from a cold. Surely it was coronavirus? OK. Then I would be next.

I had been following the news quite closely. I obsess about the things I fear: I try to know them. By the time you had both recovered I was grimly fixated by the magnitude of what seemed to be unfolding across the world. I fussed and worried. I continued my manic period of research. I took Vitamin D and Vitamin C, and avoided alcohol. Virologists and epidemiologists were warning of societal and economic collapse if swift action was not taken. It was not taken. The reality of the pandemic's arrival and what it meant for society spread through the general population far more slowly than the virus itself.

My own version of the virus never materialised, at least not beyond the usual symptoms of being run down: three mouth ulcers that refused to disappear, deep exhaustion by 7 p.m., a sore throat coming and going . . . but nothing to conclusively say I had it. It was strange. You can only read yourself for symptoms for so long, before the diagnostic prodding and swallowing becomes more of an imposition on your life than any of the minor variations in your physical state that you find yourself obsessing about. It was tiring and so I gave up, resigned to the idea, thinking, Fine, if you're coming you're coming and there's nothing I can do about it. A dread descended, I mooched and sighed. Your mother said that living with me in that state was more hard work than if I were bedridden. I agreed. I was bored of waiting and decided to stop. Life resumed. I started inventing cocktails in the evening with whatever scraps of booze we had lying around, and I named them after poets, 'The Ruefle' and 'The Teddy Roethke'.

I finished the cheap brandy from the Christmas cake and made a serious dent in the sickly, two-year-old damson vodka. I stopped worrying and started running in the evenings, listening to sugary pop songs, feeling young and gamine. I felt calm and more attentive to the present, having stopped gazing into a hypothetical convalescent future. I stopped building it up as if it were a large piece of furniture that always needed pushing across the room. I rolled from hour to hour. I was just as uncertain as before, but I had suspended my judgement and I lived habitually. *Ataraxia*. A happy shadow.

Then lockdown eased. A contradiction in terms. A gnawing dissonance. We went to the beach and it was spacious, it was heaven to be outside, but something felt tetchy ... there almost was a little static on the wind. Now it's September, and case numbers are rising again. Town feels weird. Every transaction is slightly too tentative or lurching. People seem overly relaxed or not relaxed enough. I take you to the park now the swings are back in action, and watch you lick the handrail at the top of the slide, and I have no idea what to think about it.

*

No one knows what will happen. What do we know? Humans will die out. What else do we expect – 99.9% of species do, and we can't live for ever. The permafrost is already melting, and if that accelerates ... I don't know ... but I think about it a lot. I think about my complicity. I imagine you asking me why we did not do more. I worry that you will live to see so much more mass death in your lifetime. Nine hundred thousand Covid-19 deaths this summer and counting. What will happen as climate change gets worse, and more of the world becomes inhabitable? Research conducted by the British environmentalist Norman Myers suggests that by 2050 there will be as many as 250 million climate change refugees, displaced by desertification, lack of water, the salination of farmland and the depletion of biodiversity.

The human species is numerous, and widely distributed. This is testament to our adaptability to different and extreme environments. We also have an incredibly varied diet, and we can synthesise nutrients and create or cultivate the conditions for food production instead of relying solely on its natural occurrence. However, we are relatively slow to reproduce, and as we live longer lives we are also slowing the rate at which we evolve across generations. This means we are ill set-up to adapt to the environmental changes that are occurring and are likely to occur in the future. And while we are more successful at changing our immediate environments and making them habitable, the opposite appears to be true on a larger scale.

If the question of our extinction is *how* rather than *when*, the question of our long-term survival is *who*: who will possess the technology and resources to adapt to climate change and other challenges, and how will we organise ourselves so that they might be distributed fairly? At the moment it looks grim. Insularity, nationalism, wilful ignorance and denial.

There is a map I like to look at, devised by the international relations expert Parag Khanna, which shows what the world might look like four degrees warmer. On the one hand, it is chilling. From Portland to New York there is only uninhabitable desert; China and southern Asia are also entirely desert, and so is nearly all of southern Europe, and all of Africa bar a large band stretching inwards from the west coast which can potentially be reforested. Most of South America is desert, or else uninhabitable due to extreme weather phenomena, as is the case with the Himalayas. But there are belts of green across the top of the world, where food can be grown and where our descendants

154

might live in huge mega-cities. In western Antarctica and New Zealand, too, there is a chance for human life to continue. The desert regions will not simply be wasteland either, in Khanna's vision, but instead vast areas of land will be used to house solar energy farms, and it will also be possible to generate geothermic energy in many of the areas where the weather otherwise makes living impossible. Wind farms populate the newly drawn coast-line of eastern Britain, and also off the coastlines of Canada and Patagonia. For all the violent upheaval and suffering that the map implies – the fall of nations, the collapse of the world's current superpowers – it is at least a feasible future. Siberian tomatoes and Alaskan vineyards ... perhaps a mandatory tour of service tending to the solar panels of Old Marrakech or the place they still call 'Sunset Boulevard'.

*

In the house of knowledge I defer
to my thermostat.
There is legroom all around me
to recline and find my feet.
The street outside used to be a runway
once, and on clear days the sky
still looks traumatised, as we sip
our orange juice, fresh
from the finest groves in Moscow.
I believe in my habits. I'm calm.
My body, and its shadow falling after.
This house,
and its shadow house falling.

*

I had a dream. It was early on in the pandemic, and, I don't know, maybe I hadn't processed what was going on properly during my conscious waking hours. We were living by the sea in the dream – we had planned to move to the coast this summer, but then everything got fucked up; perhaps that's why the dream was set there. There was an emergency broadcast, a government text on our phones (you were older, perhaps fifteen, you had a phone), and it said to stay indoors, but instead we rushed outside to see. And out over the sea – our house was on a cliff – was a huge bank of orange cloud, a dust or fall-out, or insects, or just bad, bad shit. We looked at each other as if to say, Oh no, this is real, this is how it ends, and your face (God, I wish I could remember what you looked like in the dream), your face was just collapsing with the grief of it, as if you were being told that everything had been a lie, that the long life you had been sold and told to prepare for, and which you had given your heart to, wept for, worked towards, was gone now. And I took you by the shoulders in the dream, and I said,

> Look at me. Look
> at me. It's OK.
> Listen. This looks
> bad and I think
> we're all going to
> die now. But you
> have to try and
> forget the future.
> That's gone. I'm
> so sorry. If I
> could give you my
> time, the time I
> had, instead, I
> would, but I just
> think it's really so
> remarkable that

we got to be here,
and to have lived
at all, and you,
god I didn't
expect you at all I
really had no idea
that you would be
a person, even
more real than me
you are . . .

And I smiled at you then and laughed, and you laughed
too. I said,

It's nothing new
what's coming
It's always been
there and I will try
to eat most of it.
*Dad you can't eat it
all.* I'm not saying
I can, I'm just
saying if you go
indoors now
and hide with
your mum, I'll eat
as much as I can.
I'll give you a
head start. OK?

. . .

I want to do it.
There's nothing I

want more.
I feel so lucky to
have met you.

And we were both crying, and then you ran back to the house . . . and so I turned and faced the cloud. It was huge and my face was fizzy, and my eyes were aching and I could feel my throat begin to burn and the dark sea rose up and got stuck, it was so unnatural and awful to see it stuck upright, like a broken bone. But I let it come and it was just a few feet away, I knew my eyes were bleeding, and all over it really started to hurt and so I fell down and curled into a ball and I cried out, and felt a jolt like an electric shock, and then there was darkness all around. I sat up into the darkness. The cat on the end of the bed stirred and began to wash loudly. The moon was bright through the blind. My heart was racing. I got out of bed and went for a wee and the air was cold on my body, with its film of sweat. I crossed the landing to your door, and listened in, waiting and waiting for a break in the traffic, but there was a run of cars or trucks, I remember it took so long, maybe the rest of my life, before I caught the sound of your breath, stopped holding my own.

*

Daddy I'm a bit bored
Life, friends, is boring . . . we must not say so . . .
What are you saying?
. . . the great sea yearns . . .
Why are you doing that funny voice Daddy?
we ourselves flash and yearn!
Daddy what are you saying?
I'm saying a poem. By John Berryman.
What is a poem?
It's a . . . Good question.

*

158

I am used to talking about poems: what they are for and what they do and how they do it. I generalise too much, and I get a little evangelical. I want people to enjoy what I enjoy and give themselves permission to find consolation in confusion, or an answer in a question, or a feeling in a song. I think that the dissonant, unruly, uncertain knowledge that poems can hold are a safe harbour from the reductive demand to know you mind, to make your mind up, to make a claim, to claim a position. It is easy to have a view if you simplify, erase, ignore and silence. A poem is a refusal to do so. It is an attempt to reclaim all that we lose to habit, to fatigue, to competition and productivity; it accommodates the errant and disobedient impulse or connection, it centres our marginalia, foregrounds the edges of the frame, white chickens, wet branches, motes and light-play, offcuts, strays, dead circuit boards, terms and names and effluents, awkward gestures, the adult timbre of a saxophone, language and language and language, and life collaged and collated. It just lets you have more, keep more.

Poets are not special people. They don't experience things with a greater intensity of feeling, or have more incisive, interesting thoughts. But they do write poems.

I don't expect you'll be a poet. I'm bound to put you off the idea, though I hope you read poems, and love them, and use them to have and keep more of your life and know the world with a greater complexity by their uncertain way of holding, weighing, leaning and asking for your participation. Mainly I want you to know that poetry is not a frivolous hobby, a luxurious kind of sentimental gesturing towards yourself and your experiences, but the most deliberate and self-aware form of the poetic, an intrinsic feature of thought and language and cognition. The poetic is a fundamental instrument of presence, of being and knowing. You're *here*. We're of its machinery, we're drowned in the barrel.

I'm not being grand. The word is not the thing, the thought is not the thing, the thing is not the thing, at least not the way you know it. There is always metaphor, representation, creative foreshortening and equivalence. And the poetic refuses to deny it. You can follow every course of logic and eventually it reaches the edge of its system, numbers referring to more numbers, values corroding towards an endless inward measurement. An awareness of those edges, the limits of the system, only situates you within it more honestly and more fully. You're so *here* now. And I don't mourn your cognitive wastefulness. I know that the further you travel into knowledge and language and reason the more inevitably you will discover their edges, their frailty and hopeful uncertainty, so often hidden from view.

Today, I got your big notebook out to see what letters your mum had taught you. Carefully, you drew a circle. *O*, you said. Good! Then you drew a vertical line, and a dot above it. Then you looked up at me and shouted *Oi!* Your first written word. I hadn't known about this development. Your mother hadn't told me. Oi! As if writing had ignored you long enough, as if you were elbowing your way into conversation.

Maybe that's what a poem is, an *Oi!* hailing us, Hey! Look! Stop! Here! This! Me!, A voice breaking through, both singular and constituent; a plea, not just for attention, but to be attentive.

*

If I sit still I can follow my mind down
a nice long corridor. Coffee tastes bad, it's true,
but it becomes so delicious to suffer it.
You will find that everything you love
you love poetically. You have to replace
it with itself so you can see it again.
Dissonance, equivocality, inflections rising
and falling. A word pressed more firmly

160

into context with a novel exactitude;
a hand offered in place of a frozen lake
is still a hand; the sound of a phrase
occupying its shape as if sprung from
the mould that history poured it into.
Emitting light, you are more alert
in a forest clearing, your senses
showing their working, thoughts
progressing like a shirt being buttoned
from the collar down. Have more.
Keep more, daughter.
Like the sandcastle when I slid the bucket
back on top and said, Where has it gone?
And you laughed a little nervously
at the new-game feel of it and when
I lifted up the bucket again, *ta-dah!*
the castle was the same, but Oi!
Look! I replaced it with itself.
And while it stood, it stood for more.
And where it stood for more,
there, still, there it stands.

DETAILS OF WORKS CITED

pp. 8, 69, 70, George Lakoff and Rafael E. Núñez, *Where Mathematics Comes From: How the Embodied Mind Brings Mathematics into Being* (Basic Books, 2000).

p. 9, Alfred Korzybski, *Science and Sanity: An Introduction to Non-Aristotelian Systems and General Semantics* (Institute of General Semantics, 1995).

p. 11, Henri Bergson, *Creative Evolution*, trans. Arthur Mitchell (Gray Rabbit, 2019).

p. 14, William Shakespeare, *Hamlet*, Act V, Scene 2, *The Complete Works*, Stanley Wells and Gary Taylor, eds (OUP, 1986).

p. 15, John Keats, 'On Negative Capability: Letter to George and Tom Keats, 21, 27? December 1817' *Keats's Poetry and Prose* (Norton critical editions, 2009).

pp. 15, 63, 64, 66 & 113, Lorraine Code, *What Can She Know? Feminist Theory and the Construction of Knowledge* (Cornell University Press, 1991).

p. 16, Wolfgang Iser, 'The Reading Process: A Phenomenological Approach', *New Literary History*, vol. 3, no. 2 (Winter 1972).

p. 18, Federico García Lorca, 'Song of the Motionless Gardener', *Suites*, trans. Jerome Rothenberg (Green Integer, 2000).

pp. 27, 71, 84, Carlo Rovelli, *Seven Brief Lessons On Physics* (Penguin, 2016).

p. 28, Michio Kaku, 'Who's Afraid of a Big Black Hole', *Horizon*, BBC Television (2010).

p. 30, *New Scientist*, 'Black Hole Breakthrough: A Lot Done, Much More to Do', no. 3226 (April 2019).

p. 32, Helen Castor, *Joan of Arc: A History* (Harper Perennial, 2016).

p. 41, Elizabeth Barret Browning, *Aurora Leigh* (www.poetry-foundation.org/poems/145567/aurora-leigh-book-1).

pp. 41, 44, Richard Feynman, *The Feynman Lectures on Physics*, vol. 3 (www.feynmanlectures.caltech.edu).

p. 48, Max Planck, 'Letter to Robert W. Wood: 7 October 1931', in *Theoretical Concepts in Physics: An Alternative View of Theoretical Reasoning in Physics*, Professor Malcolm S Longair (Cambridge, 2003) p339.

p. 48, Albert Einstein, 'On a Heuristic Viewpoint Concerning the Production and Transformation of Light' (people.isy.liu.se/jalar/kurser/QF/references/Einstein1905b.pdf).

p. 49, W. H. Auden, 'The Virgin and the Dynamo', *The Dyer's Hand: And Other Essays* (Faber & Faber, 1963).

p. 51, Daniel Hobbins, *The Trial of Joan of Arc*, new edn (Harvard University Press, 2007).

p. 71, Eugene Wigner, 'The Unreasonable Effectiveness of Mathematics in the Natural Sciences' (www.dartmouth.edu/~matc/MathDrama/reading/Wigner.html).

p. 78, Ray Kurzweil, *The Singularity is Near* (Duckworth, 2006).

p. 79, Donna Haraway, *A Cyborg Manifesto: Science, Technology, and Socialist-Feminism in the Late Twentieth Century* (University of Minnesota Press, 2016).

p. 80, Jillian Weise, 'Common Cyborg', *Granta Magazine*, 24 September 2018 (www.granta.com/common-cyborg).

p. 81, 'The Artificial Pancreas', De Montfort University website

(www.dmu.ac.uk/research/research-faculties-and-institutes/
health-and-life-sciences/pharmaceutical-technologies/research-
projects/artificial-pancreas/the-artificial-pancreas.aspx).

p. 82, Saint Augustine, *Confessions*, trans. R. S. Pine-Coffin
(Penguin, 1961).

p. 84, Michael Haneke, dir., *Amour* (Les films du lozange, 2012)
[trans. author's own].

p. 96, Albert Einstein, 'Letter to Besso Family: Spring 1955', 'Time's
arrow: Albert Einstein's letters to Michele Besso' (https://
www.christies.com/features/Einstein-letters-to-Michele-
Besso-8422-1.aspx).

p. 102, Henri Bergson, 'Duration and Simultaneity: With Reference
to Einstein's Theory', trans. Leon Jacobson (The Library of
Liberal Arts, 1965).

p. 102, Svante Arrhenius, Presentation Speech for the 1921 Nobel
Prize in Physics, 10 December 1922, The Nobel Prize (www.
nobelprize.org/prizes/physics/1921/ceremony-speech).

p. 104, Elizabeth Bishop, 'In the Waiting Room', *Complete Poems*
(Chatto & Windus, 2004).

p. 112, C. W. Chou et al., 'Optical Clocks and Relativity',
Science, vol. 329, no. 5999 (September 2010), 1630–33.

p. 113, John D. Caputo, *Truth: The Search for Wisdom in the
Postmodern Age* (Penguin, 2013.

p. 117, Mingbo Cai, David M. Eagleman, and Wei Ji Ma, 'Perceived
Duration Is Reduced by Repetition But Not by High-Level
Expectation', *Journal of Vision*, vol. 15, no. 13 (September 2015).

p. 117, Mohammad Ali Nazari et al., 'Time Dilation Caused by
Oddball Serial Position and Pitch Deviancy: A Comparison
of Musicians and Nonmusicians', *Music Perception*, vol. 35,
no. 4 (April 2018), 425–36.

p. 124, Office for National Statistics, Household debt in
Great Britain April 2016 to March 2018, taken from the

sixth round of the Wealth and Assets Survey (https://www.ons.gov.uk/peoplepopulationandcommunity/personalandhouseholdfinances/incomeandwealth/bulletins/householddebtingreatbritain/april2016tomarch2018).

p. 125, Naomi I. Eisenberger, Matthew D. Lieberman and Kipling D. Williams, 'Does Rejection Hurt? An fMRI Study of Social Exclusion', *Science*, vol. 302, no. 5643 (October 2003), 290–92.

p. 126, Keise Izuma, Daisuke N. Saito and Norihiro Sadato, 'Processing of Social and Monetary Rewards in the Human Striatum', *Neuron*, vol. 58, no. 2 (April 2008), 284–94.

pp. 127, 128, 129, 131, 133 & 134, Marieke de Goede, *Virtue, Fortune and Faith: A Genealogy of Finance* (University of Minnesota Press, 2005).

p. 133, Franco 'Bifo' Berardi, *The Uprising: On Poetry and Finance* (Semiotext(e), 2012).

p. 136, Andrea Brady, 'The Determination of Love', *Journal of the British Academy*, vol. 5 (2017), 271–308.

p. 142, Gilles Deleuze and Félix Guattari, *A Thousand Plateaus: Capitalism and Schizophrenia*, trans. Brian Massumi (Continuum, 2004).

p. 142, Mikhail Bakhtin, *Rabelais and His World*, trans. Hélène Iswolsky (Indiana University Press, 2009).

p. 149, Harald Thorsrud, 'Ancient Greek Skepticism', *Internet Encyclopedia of Philosophy* (www.iep.utm.edu/skepanci).

p. 153, Norman Myers, 'Environmental Refugees in a Globally Warmed World', *BioScience*, vol. 43, no. 11 (December 1993), 752–62.

p. 154, Parag Khanna, 'The World 4 Degrees Warmer' (www.paragkhanna.com/2016-3-9-the-world-4-degrees-warmer).

p. 158, John Berryman, 'Dream Song 14', *77 Dream Songs* (Faber & Faber, 2001).

ACKNOWLEDGEMENTS

I am grateful to the editors and staff of the following publications and organisations for publishing or supporting this book through its various drafts and versions: *The Poetry Review*, *POETRY* magazine, *PORT* and *Adbusters*; I am grateful to the Arts Foundation for my 2017 shortlisting for the Arts Foundation Creative Non-fiction Prize; I would especially like to thank Ben Pester, Max Porter, Emily Berry, Joe Dunthorne, Laura Barber and Theis Anderson for key notes and steers, and Kaveh Akbar, Samantha Harvey, Bethan Lloyd Worthington, Jane Feaver, Kathryn Maris, Ella Rimmer, Joseph Williams, Holly Pester, Naomi Wood, Nell Stevens, Mark d'Inverno, Tim Parnell, and mum and dad for timely, thoughtful and supportive noises along the way; I cannot repay Tommy Ogden enough for his enormous help with the physics but I promise to try; let the record also show that I began writing a non-fiction book because Željka Marošević suggested the idea; I would like to thank Gesche Ipsen for copy-editing this book like a great white shark; and my editor Sarah Castleton, for getting it and trusting it, and becoming such a wise and kind friend by it, too; no one has borne and aided and suffered this book more than my dear agent Harriet Moore; and no one has suffered me writing it more than Hannah Bagshaw, without whom I would have no life or daughter to speak of; and I am most grateful to Nancy, for all of herself.